The Nine Commandments

THE ANCHOR BIBLE REFERENCE LIBRARY is designed to be a third major component of the Anchor Bible group, which includes the Anchor Bible commentaries on the books of the Old Testament, the New Testament, and the Apocrypha, and the Anchor Bible Dictionary. While the Anchor Bible commentaries and the Anchor Bible Dictionary are structurally defined by their subject matter, the Anchor Bible Reference Library will serve as a supplement on the cutting edge of the most recent scholarship. The series is open-ended; its scope and reach are nothing less than the biblical world in its totality, and its methods and techniques the most up-to-date available or devisable. Separate volumes will deal with one or more of the following topics relating to the Bible: anthropology, archaeology, ecology, economy, geography, history, languages and literatures, philosophy, religion(s), theology.

As with the Anchor Bible commentaries and the Anchor Bible Dictionary, the philosophy underlying the Anchor Bible Reference Library finds expression in the following: the approach is scholarly, the perspective is balanced and fair-minded, the methods are scientific, and the goal is to inform and enlighten. Contributors are chosen on the basis of their scholarly skills and achievements, and they come from a variety of religious backgrounds and communities. The books in the Anchor Bible Reference Library are intended for the broadest possible readership, ranging from world-class scholars, whose qualifications match those of the authors, to general readers, who may not have special training or skill in studying the Bible but are as enthusiastic as any dedicated professional in expanding their knowledge of the Bible and its world.

David Noel Freedman
GENERAL EDITOR

THE ANCHOR BIBLE REFERENCE LIBRARY

THE NINE COMMANDMENTS

Uncovering a Hidden Pattern of
Crime and Punishment in the Hebrew Bible

DAVID NOEL FREEDMAN

with
JEFFREY C. GEOGHEGAN *and* MICHAEL M. HOMAN
edited by ASTRID B. BECK

ABRL

DOUBLEDAY

NEW YORK   LONDON   TORONTO   SYDNEY   AUCKLAND

THE ANCHOR BIBLE REFERENCE LIBRARY
PUBLISHED BY DOUBLEDAY
a division of Random House, Inc.
1540 Broadway, New York, New York 10036

THE ANCHOR BIBLE REFERENCE LIBRARY, DOUBLEDAY,
and the portrayal of an anchor with the letters ABRL
are trademarks of Doubleday, a division of Random House, Inc.

Book design by Fearn Cutler de Vicq de Cumptich

The Library of Congress has catalogued the Doubleday
hardcover edition as follows:
Freedman, David Noel, 1922–
The nine commandments: uncovering a hidden pattern of crime and
punishment in the Hebrew Bible / by David Noel Freedman; with Jeffrey C.
Geoghegan and Michael M. Homan; edited by Astrid Billes Beck.—1st ed.
p.   cm.
Includes bibliographical references and index.
1. Ten commandments.   2. Crime in the Bible.   3. Bible. O.T.—Criticism,
interpretation, etc.   I. Geoghegan, Jeffrey C.   II. Homan, Michael M.
III. Beck, Astrid B.   IV. Title.
BS1285.2 F74 2000
222′.1606—dc21   00-029492

ISBN 0-385-49987-6

PRINTED IN THE UNITED STATES OF AMERICA
1   3   5   7   9   10   8   6   4   2

Contents

List of Illustrations

Preface

The idea or theme underlying *The Nine Commandments* originated with my discovery that the central or major narrative of the Hebrew Bible beginning at the beginning of the Book of Genesis continued in estimable fashion all the way through the Book(s) of Kings, where it ended with the capture of Jerusalem, the destruction of the Temple, and the captivity of the Jewish people. The formal division between Torah (the first five books) and the Former Prophets (the next four books) was artificial and dictated by nonliterary, theopolitical considerations.

While the theme is in itself rather simple and transparent, nevertheless it runs counter to the prevailing trends in critical historical literary scholarship, which has been dedicated largely to the analysis and isolation of the component strands of this admittedly composite work, and where attention has been concentrated on individual strands (i.e., J, E, D, P) and on partial assemblages or building blocks which formally make up the whole (which I call the Primary History), i.e., Tetrateuch, Hexateuch, Deuteronomic History, along with the traditional Pentateuch and Former Prophets.

While the observation is self-evident and requires only the listing of the constituent parts in the order in which they occur in the Hebrew Bible, it is at least prudent if not obligatory in this case to support the claim with data and coherent argument. Thus

I thought it useful to show how the front and the back, the beginning and the end of the story fit together, forming a tightly sealed envelope around the whole historiographic mass of details between Genesis and 2 Kings, in particular, how a hearer or reader at the end of the story, a Jewish exile in Babylon, might read the opening narratives at the beginning of the story in Genesis (2–4), in which the original inhabitants of the Garden of Eden, after being apprised of the rules and being warned of the consequences, nevertheless disobeyed their creator and were punished by being thrown out of their homeland. In the second story (Cain and Abel), the brother who also violated the rules was punished by being driven into exile. In a nutshell, these stories summarize the experience of all Israel as recounted in the Primary History, and the perceptive reader would recognize from the start the drift and tenor, the direction and endpoint of the entire narrative.

By way of reinforcement of the thesis, I also pointed to the last of these introductory narratives: the story of Babel (the city) and its tower. It was from Babel that the human race was dispersed over the earth, and importantly, among those who joined the migration were the direct ancestors of the patriarchs and their descendants, the people of Israel. After being mentioned early in Genesis, Babylon (Babel) disappears from view entirely until the end of the narrative in 2 Kings, where it surfaces as the final destination of the surviving remnant of the people of Israel. They have come full circle: from Babylon to Babylon.

Having established the link between beginning and end, I thought that it would help to settle the case and cement the sequence to find evidence of the continuity in the narrative beyond and more striking than a mere chronological string, in itself not a small point, that with few interruptions or backtracking, the story line runs in consecutive fashion. Early on, I was struck by the centrality and incisive importance of the Decalogue in its larger context. Not only was it the heart of the covenant between God and Israel, as mediated by that all-important figure Moses, but it pro-

vided the key items, the flashpoints in the ongoing historical interaction between deity and people. Immediately apparent was
the fact that Israel's historical experience would be defined by its
response to the terms of the covenant, specifically how it dealt
with the violations of the commandments. The very dramatic stories of David's adultery, and the appalling behavior of Ahab and
Jezebel in the murder and dispossession of Naboth, illustrated
vividly the downward spiral that began with the radical rebellion
against commandment, covenant, and God himself in the days immediately following the solemn ratification of the covenant in the
episode of the Golden Calf (Exod 19–24, 32–34).

Gradually, it became clear to me that within the larger and
more general patterns in which the decline and fall of Israel (including Judah) are told, a more precise and detailed correlation
exists between the commandments and the books—tracing the
progress or regress of Israel from independence and nationhood
to disaster in the loss of freedom, kingdom, and land. In the end,
I was able to formulate the process in the following way.

Beginning with the declaration of the Decalogue and the seal-
ing of the covenant, the story of Israel would bear out the solemn
warnings provided by Moses in his farewell speech in Deuteronomy: persistent violation of the covenant would result in the destruction of the nation. As it happens, by their violation of each
commandment—one by one, book by book—until they run out
of both books and commandments, they seal their doom. By then
they are back in Babylon where they started, having lost everything that had been given to them by a kind, gracious, merciful
God, who nevertheless insists on behavior worthy of the chosen
people. For the "missing" commandment, you will have to read
the book.

I am deeply grateful to a number of people for the accomplish-
ment of this task. If the original idea and the form in which it has
been presented are my responsibility, the finished work owes much
to many helping hands. The chapters on the individual commandments were prepared by Jeffrey Geoghegan and Michael Homan.

Astrid Beck assembled and edited the entire work. Susan Friedman researched and supplied the illustrations used. Andrew Corbin, Editor at Doubleday, guided the book through all its critical phases to final and present publication. I owe a debt of thanks to Eric Major, Director of Religious Publishing at Doubleday, for his commitment to and confidence in the author(s) and this undertaking.

David Noel Freedman
June 24, 2000

Foreword

————◆✦◆————

The seeds for this book, *The Nine Commandments,* were sown long ago. The topic of the commandments has preoccupied David Noel Freedman throughout his long, productive, and creative scholarly career. We can see formative renderings of his concept in his early writings, for example in his treatise "The Unity of the Bible" (1956). Though the orientation of that article is theological, he discusses the idea of covenant and adherence to the commandments:

> We may conclude the discussion of the framework of biblical unity with the **Covenant**, the bond between God and his community.[1]

In 1991, he delivered the prestigious Mowinkel Lecture at the University of Oslo entitled "The Symmetry of the Hebrew Bible."[2] This treatise is mathematical in approach, and includes much detailed work on syllable and word counts. It is a precise analysis, based on numerical data, to prove the case for a Master Editor of the Hebrew Bible. In between, he published his famous article in *Bible Review,* "The Nine Commandments: The Secret Progress of Israel's Sins" (1989).[3] This article was based on his Distinguished Faculty Lectureship series at the University of Michigan in March 1988. The lectures were later published in a small volume.[4]

The subject of the commandments is intrinsically intriguing.

They are a puzzle, and puzzles are David Noel Freedman's favorite pastime. And like a puzzle, there is a catch, a surprise component that is integral to it. The idea of covenant and commandment, transgression and sin, is a thread that runs through the entire biblical narrative. The penalty for transgression is death, as pronounced early in Genesis. But God often mitigates the punishment, for he takes pity on his creation. And so the punishment is generally exile. One of the nuggets buried deep in the Commentary on Amos is Freedman's excursus "When God Repents."[5] It is an eloquent exposition of the verb *nḥm*, to repent, to change one's mind, and details the history of the Hebrew word in the narrative of the Hebrew Bible when God repents and then changes his mind over his decision to destroy his people for their transgressions. In the excursus, David Noel Freedman states:

> Divine repentance can move in either of two directions: from judgment to clemency or the other way around. It can also move in both directions sequentially . . . from judgment to forgiveness and then back to judgment . . . Throughout and in every case, it should be understood that the divine repentance is real; that the meaning and value of the story depend on the transaction between God and prophet, or God and people . . . Admittedly we are using a metaphor, involving stories and persons that include God and humans; but within the metaphor . . . we must be faithful to the data. Once it is understood that Yahweh enters into the drama as fully and wholeheartedly as the other participants, then we can proceed with the analysis . . . The first example to claim our attention is at the beginning of the Flood Story in Gen 6:6–7 (J). We read: "and Yahweh repented (= regretted, *wayyinnāḥem*) that he had made mankind on the earth, and he afflicted himself to his heart." . . . The decision based on the change of will, and the pain and agony of the act of reversal of previous decisions and acts, are expressed sharply by the use of a remarkable *hitpaᶜel* form from the root ᶜṣb,

which means literally that he inflicted pain on himself (= he tortured himself or he agonized); the added phrase "to his heart [= mind]," only strengthens the force of the affliction. Coming to a new decision was no light matter; it involved an agonizing reappraisal (as the expression goes) and was reached with great personal pain.[6]

The excursus is a remarkable treatise on God's repentance and forgiveness that spans the biblical narrative much as does the account of these nine commandments. David Noel Freedman's thesis, as outlined in *The Unity of the Hebrew Bible,* is to view the structure of the biblical narrative as largely

> pyramidal and symmetric; . . . like a domed building in which the apex is near or at the center, and the opening and closing form a ring or pair of interlocking parts that constitute the foundation. For the Hebrew Bible as a whole, the center comes at the end of the Primary History and at the beginning of the Latter Prophets—at which point the Bible tells of the captivity of the people of Judah, the loss of nationhood, and the destruction of the capital city of Jerusalem and the Temple . . . We can say, therefore, that the entire Hebrew Bible revolves around the point in time, that historical moment when the life of the nation came to an end, when tragedy struck in multiple blows at the kingdom, at its ruling dynasty, and at the sacred center of worship and service of their God.[7]

God is the central and dominant figure of the whole story and the entire Bible. But Freedman makes a persuasive case that the Bible is also a series of successive parables of human disobedience and depravity that leads to the necessary consequences in punishment, banishment, and exile. It begins with the story of Adam and Eve, the story of disobedience and rebellion against the commandment of God, in the Garden of Eden. The upshot of that story is banishment from the Garden to the life of exile in the world.

Freedman poses the question: "How could those in captivity in Babylon . . . miss the point or fail to compare the story in Genesis with theirs?"[8]

They were back in Babel, the city of Babylon, the same point where Abraham, their revered ancestor, began the journey. It must have seemed like a retrograde journey to those deprived of their freedom and their independence. Freedman calls this account the Primary History. He says:

> So far as I am aware, it is the first and perhaps the most important and influential prose narrative ever written, preceding, for example, Herodotus and his *History of the Persian Wars* by at least a century. The Primary History may be compared with such a historical work because it constitutes historical writing . . .[9]

He connects the comparison to the great epic poetry of the *Iliad* and *Odyssey,* and before that, the cycle of poems associated with Gilgamesh and Enkidu. One might include the *Aeneid* as well. Central in all the stories is the fall of the capital city and the accompanying collapse of a dynasty and kingdom. In the biblical account, the story is clearly told from the perspective of the losers, its emphasis the pervasive note of tragedy. The central event is the giving of the commandments, the ratification of the covenant. At the midpoint, the heart, of the Primary History, in the Book of Deuteronomy, Moses recalls for the listener the stirring events on the sacred mountain forty years earlier. In the transgression of the commandments, the community is held responsible for these transgressions. Recitation, repetition, is to reinforce the message for the listener.

Freedman makes a convincing case that the neat fit is the work of a Master Editor/Redactor, of a guiding editorial hand, "an individual who is anonymous to us, but certainly a real person with a name and a calling, who richly deserves the honor of recognition for compiling and producing the first full-scale history of a nation."[10] Freedman's students will also recognize his points on parallel construction and envelope construction in these narratives. He, the archetypal and master editor of the most distinguished critical commentary series, as also of numerous other series in the field, should know the role of master editor.

A colleague from Michigan, the greatly esteemed anthropologist, Roy A. Rappaport, paid tribute to David Noel Freedman, when he wrote:

> David Noel Freedman's life has been devoted to the illumination of words of the Hebrew Bible in all their dimensions and through all their scales—from the spelling of individual words, the shaping of those words into poetry, the grand but previously unnoticed symmetries underlying the structure of *Tanakh* in its entirety, to, finally, the ordering of all those scriptural words into the Word of the Hebrew God. Nor has he confined himself to Scripture per se. He has also been concerned with how its Word has been lived in the communities it has defined and guided, particularly the community of ancient Israel.[11]

Roy Rappaport called Noel the foremost scribe since Ezra, and this not so much in jest. This book represents the culmination of David Noel Freedman's theories on biblical elucidation and editorship. He has been ably assisted by his two collaborators, Jeff Geoghegan and Mike Homan, his students at the University of California, San Diego. They have worked through the treatise and given it the scribal polish in the ancient tradition of Baruch, Jeremiah's scribe. We acknowledge their erudition and excellent skills.

It has been my good fortune and great honor to work with David Noel Freedman on many projects for more than fifteen years. The collaboration has been challenging and fun.

Astrid Billes Beck
Ann Arbor, Michigan
November 1999

The Nine Commandments

Introduction

———◆◆◆◆◆———

Hidden in the Bible is a previously unrecognized pattern of commandment violations, a pattern that has gone undetected for more than two thousand years. In the books spanning Exodus to Kings, the nation of Israel is presented to the reader as thoroughly defying its covenant with God by breaking each of the Ten Commandments, one by one, book by book, in order, until there are none—leaving God with only one choice: the destruction of the nation. After the last commandment is broken, the nation finds itself living on borrowed time. First the northern kingdom (called Israel) in 722 B.C.E. and then the southern kingdom (called Judah) in 586 B.C.E. is destroyed by the Assyrian and Babylonian armies, respectively. Upon the defeat of the southern kingdom, Jerusalem is razed, the Temple, the very dwelling place of God, is destroyed, and the survivors, God's "chosen people," are exiled, no longer to live securely in their "Promised Land."

The pages that follow will trace the hidden trail of sin, this scarlet thread of commandment violations running through the tapestry of Israel's history. What we will discover is that the presence of this thread betrays the hand of a Master Weaver or Editor who has skillfully woven into Israel's history a message to a community in exile that their present condition is not the result of God abandoning them, but of their abandoning God through their complete disregard for their covenant obligations as embodied in the Ten Commandments. I trust that the journey of un-covering this hidden thread will be as gripping to read as it is ex-citing to explore.

"In the Beginning . . ."

The pattern of *command* → *command violation* → *exile* appears early in the biblical record—in fact, it shows up "in the beginning." Shortly after creating Adam, God gives him what would be hu-mankind's first command:[1]

> From every tree of the garden you may certainly eat, but from the tree of the knowledge of good and evil you may not eat, for in the day that you eat from it you will certainly die.
>
> GENESIS 2:16B–17

Even if one has never read or heard this story before, the out-come is easy to predict. Adam and Eve, in defiance of God's com-mand, eat of the forbidden fruit.

Realizing now that they are naked, they cover themselves with leaves. However, their unclad condition would soon be the least of their worries:

> Then they heard the sound of Yahweh God walking in the garden in the breeze of the day, and Adam and his wife hid themselves from the presence of Yahweh God among the trees in the garden.
>
> GENESIS 3:8

There is, of course, no hiding from God. And even though God asks Adam and Eve, "Where are you?"[2] we know from this narrative's companion tale, the murder of Abel by Cain, that such questions are more a test of the individual being questioned than a fact-finding mission on the part of God.

After Cain has killed his brother, God inquires, "Where is Abel, your brother?"[3] Cain, presumably believing that God really doesn't know and that he can hide the truth from God, plays innocent:

I don't know. Am I my brother's keeper?

GENESIS 4:9B

God's response reveals the rhetorical nature of his initial question to Cain regarding Abel's whereabouts:

What have you done? [Another rhetorical question.] The voice of your brother's blood is crying out to me from the ground!

GENESIS 4:10

Cain, like his parents in the Garden, is caught. And though Adam is more forthcoming with the facts than his son (Adam: "I was afraid because I am naked, and I hid myself"; Cain: "I don't know"), Adam still attempts to skirt responsibility in the matter. When asked by God if he had eaten of the forbidden fruit, Adam protests,

The woman, whom *you* gave to be with me, *she* gave to me from the tree and I ate.

GENESIS 3:12

It is as though Adam is saying, "God, *you* gave me the woman who, in turn, gave me the fruit! Therefore, *you* are the one to blame! But if *you* aren't, then *she* is, since she gave me the fruit! Whatever the case, it wasn't my fault!" Perhaps to Adam's amazement, God *does* turn to Eve and ask, "What is this you have done?"

Eve, who similarly does not want to be implicated in this crime, passes the buck once more:

The serpent deceived me, and I ate!

GENESIS 3:13

Richard Elliott Friedman, a colleague at the University of California, San Diego, and author of the best-selling book *Who Wrote the Bible?*, has jokingly suggested that if there had been another animal within "blaming distance," then the serpent would have gestured to it and said, "The dog, which *you* created, he tricked me into deceiving the woman, and so I did!" The point is well taken. This blame game is just postponing the inevitable, and in reverse order, from snake to Eve to Adam, God punishes or "curses" each of the accomplices.

The serpent will forever go about on its belly and eat the dust of the earth. Moreover, there will always be enmity between the serpent and its descendants and the woman and her descendants.

The woman will forever experience pain in childbirth. Moreover, in a statement that has resulted in considerable discussion and debate as to its exact meaning, God says to Eve, "Your desire will be for your husband and he will rule over you."[4] (Perhaps the explanation for patriarchy, perhaps not.)

The man will forever experience toil or, more literally, "pain" when working the earth. In fact, the same word used to describe the woman's pain in childbirth *('itsavon)* is used to describe the man's pain in working the soil. That is to say, just as the woman will experience pain in bringing forth the produce of the womb, so the man will experience pain in bringing forth the produce of the earth.

Then comes the promised judgment of death, though it is not immediate or "on the very day that you eat of it," as God had originally stated:

> By the sweat of your brow [literally, "nose"] you will eat bread, Until you return to the ground, for from it you were taken. For dust you are, and to dust you will return.
>
> GENESIS 3:19

Whether this "postponed" death was the original intent of God's statement that "on the day that you eat of it you will certainly die" (that is, the death process would begin on that day) or whether this is an example of God's mitigating an originally harsher sentence (from instant death to eventual death) is unclear. In support of the suggestion that God is exercising his mercy, we again refer to the companion tale of Cain and Abel. In that narrative God tells Cain that he is going to cast Cain out of his presence forever and leave him "a ceaseless wanderer on the earth."[5] Cain's appeal to God is pitiful:

> My punishment is too great for me to bear! . . . It will come about that anyone who finds me will murder me!
>
> GENESIS 4:13B, 14B

Cain has just murdered his innocent brother, yet he protests to God that his punishment is too severe because someone might murder him! Despite the irony of his concern, God acquiesces to Cain's request by placing a "mark" upon him so that anyone encountering him will not kill him.[6]

In light of God's merciful treatment of Cain despite the severity of his sin, it may be that God is being merciful to Adam and Eve as well, lessening their punishment from instantaneous death ("on the day that you eat of it") to "natural" death ("until you return to the ground"). Regardless of our conclusion on this matter, the pattern of *command* → *command violation* → *exile* is evident in both narratives.

In the case of Adam and Eve, God commands them not to eat of the tree of the knowledge of good and evil, they violate the command, and then are "exiled" from the Garden of Eden. Regarding their banishment from the Garden, the text informs us:

> And Yahweh God sent them from the Garden of Eden . . . and he *drove* the man out.
>
> GENESIS 3:23A, 24A

In the case of Cain, God warns him to control his animosity toward Abel before it is too late, Cain violates this command by murdering his brother, and then is "exiled" from the presence of God. Cain bemoans his fate with language paralleling God's treatment of Adam and Eve:[7]

> Thus, you have *driven* me this day from the face of the earth and from your face I will be hidden!
>
> GENESIS 4:14

	Command →	Violation →	Exile
Adam and Eve	"But from the tree of the knowledge of good and evil you may not eat." (GEN 2:17)	"And she took from its fruit and she ate, and she gave it also to the man with her and he ate." (GEN 3:6B)	"And Yahweh God sent him from the Garden of Eden . . . and he *drove* the man out. . ." (GEN 3:23A,24A)
Cain	"Sin is lying in wait at the door and its desire is for you, but you must master it." (GEN 4:7B)	"And Cain rose up against Abel, his brother, and killed him." (GEN 4:8B)	"Thus, you have *driven* me this day from the face of the earth and from your face I will be hidden!" (GEN 4:14)

So from the very beginning we are introduced to the theme of exile, exile that comes as the result of violating God's commands. This theme would not have been missed by the exiles reading the recently compiled history spanning Genesis to Kings, a history that begins with Adam and Eve's exile from Paradise and ends with their own exile from the Promised Land.

The Ten Commandments

In the examples above a single command is given and, once violated, the responsible party is exiled or "driven away" from the presence of God. Yet, when we come to the book of Exodus, where God establishes a covenant with the whole nation of Israel, their covenant obligations are represented by ten commandments, or "ten words" as they are referred to in the Hebrew.[8] Why ten?

While I cannot say for certain, part of the reason for ten commandments may be that when dealing with a whole nation, more chances are required; otherwise it would be a short-lived national existence if after the first violation Israel was sent into exile. But this still does not explain why there are ten commandments, and not, say, seven or twelve, numbers of comparable significance in the Bible.[9]

The reason for the connection between the number ten and the number of commandments probably has to do with a simple anatomical reality: ten is the number of fingers on the human hand. The rationale is this: once you have counted to ten, you have exhausted all of your fingers, and hence, all of your chances. In fact, that God was in the habit of giving people ten chances is seen in at least two other events in the Bible, both of which occur during the life of Moses, the mediator of the Ten Commandments.

The Ten Plagues

The story of Israel's release from Egyptian bondage is appealing in its timeless themes of freedom from slavery, liberation from oppression, and personal and national autonomy.[10] Yet, in the Exodus event this freedom comes at a high price—not so much for those who are seeking their freedom, but for those who would deny it. Egypt suffers repeatedly for the obstinate behavior of its king, the Pharaoh, who refuses to let Israel go. Warning after warning, plague after plague, Pharaoh continues to harden his heart. Not until the tenth and final plague, the most severe of them all (the death of the firstborn), does Pharaoh finally agree to release Israel. Even though many scholars today see in this narrative several different sources, each with a different number of plagues, the final form of the text gives us ten. And it is the tenth that results in the final and decisive judgment on the nation of Egypt.

That this pattern of ten is not mere coincidence is demonstrated in our next example of ten violations, which also marks the end of Yahweh's patience and results in his judgment on a nation.

Israel's Ten Rebellions

Once free from Egyptian bondage, the Israelites begin their trek to the mountain where God first appeared to Moses.[11] While they are on their way, Pharaoh has a "change of heart" and decides he must bring back the slaves he has just released.[12] Soon the Israelites find themselves trapped between the Red Sea and the Egyptian army.[13] The people, apparently forgetting that they had just been delivered from bondage via ten miraculous plagues, cry out to Moses:

> Is it because there are no graves in Egypt that you have taken us to die in the wilderness? What is this you have done to us, bringing us out of Egypt? Is not this the matter about which we spoke to you while in Egypt, saying, "Cease from us! And let us serve the Egyptians!" For it would be better for us to serve the Egyptians than for us to die in the wilderness!
>
> EXODUS 14:11–12

Talk about ingratitude. Actually, there is a degree of humor in their (rhetorical) question regarding graves in Egypt, since even to suggest that there were not enough graves in Egypt is like our suggesting that the Pope is not Catholic. Egypt was replete with burial places, pyramidal and otherwise.[14]

But neither God nor Moses is easily dissuaded by this bunch of ingrates. Moses replies,

> Do not fear! Take your stand and see the salvation of Yahweh that he will accomplish for you today. For the Egyp-

tians whom you see today, you will not see again—forever!
Yahweh will do battle for you, and as for you, be silent!

EXODUS 14:13–14

With this, God commands Moses to lift up his rod in order to split the Red Sea, providing a way of escape for the Israelites. The rest, as they say, is Hollywood. Moses leads Israel through the Red Sea upon dry ground and, once the Israelites are safely on the other side, the pursuing Egyptian army is drowned under the powerful surge of the collapsing walls of water. In response to Yahweh's miraculous deliverance, Israel sings a song of praise to him for his omnipotence and goodness.[15]

Now one would think that the ten plagues and the splitting of the Red Sea would be enough to convince the Israelites that all will be well if they just stick with Yahweh and his servant Moses. But such is not the case. No more than three days after the Red Sea incident, the Israelites are complaining to Moses again, but this time for *lack* of water.[16] God miraculously provides for them and the Israelites continue on their march toward Mount Sinai. However, a short time later Israel is grumbling once more, only this time for want of food:

What we would have given to die by the hand of Yahweh in the land of Egypt, when we sat by pots of meat, when we ate bread to the full! For you have brought us out into this wilderness to kill this whole assembly with famine.

EXODUS 16:3

Again God provides for the people, giving them "bread from heaven," or manna (meaning "What's this?" according to the narrative), and quail. Yet, not long after this event, the people are complaining again. And so the cycle continues.

Many people reading this sequence of "rapid rebellion" wonder if there is any limit to Yahweh's patience. In fact, there is—

and we discover this limit in the book of Numbers, where Israel puts God to the test one too many times.

The Limit Is Ten

In Numbers 13, God commands Moses to send spies into the land of Canaan, one spy from each of the twelve tribes of Israel. Moses, in turn, commands the spies,

> Go up this way into the Negev, and go up into the hill country, and see what the land is like, and the people dwelling in it, whether they are strong or weak, whether few or many, and whether the land in which they are dwelling is good or bad, and whether the cities in which they are dwelling are camps or fortresses, and whether the land is fertile or desolate—are there trees in it or not?
>
> NUMBERS 13:17B–20

Forty days later the spies return with produce from the land.[17] They also have some good news and some bad news. First the good news:

> We went into the land where you sent us, and it is indeed a land flowing with milk and honey—and this is its fruit!
>
> NUMBERS 13:27

Now the bad news:

> However, the people who dwell in the land are strong, and the cities are well fortified and very big. Moreover, we saw the descendants of Anak [reputed giants] there.
>
> NUMBERS 13:28

Yet, not all the spies are equally intimidated by these giants. Joshua, Moses' right-hand-man and the leader of the tribe of Ephraim, and Caleb, the leader of the tribe of Judah, think that the inhabitants of the land are no match for the Israelites, especially given Yahweh's promise of victory. Caleb quiets the murmuring crowd and says, "We will *certainly* go up and possess the land, for we are *certainly* able to do it!" (Numbers 13:30). What happens next is somewhat surprising and subtle enough to be missed if not read carefully. The ten spies, fearing that such positive talk might convince the Israelites to attempt a military campaign, revise their report by deemphasizing the fertility of the land and overemphasizing the stature of the inhabitants. They say to the people,

> The land that we traversed to spy out is a land that consumes its inhabitants! And all the people whom we saw in it were people of considerable size. And we saw the Nephilim there . . . We looked like grasshoppers in our own eyes, and we must have looked that way in their eyes as well.
>
> NUMBERS 13:32B–33

The spies say, in effect, "Did we say 'a land of fertility'? We meant 'a land of famine.' In fact, rather than its inhabitants consuming the produce of the land, the land consumes its inhabitants! And speaking of the inhabitants, when we said the descendants of Anak, we meant, more specifically, the legendary Nephilim!" Now, according to Genesis 6, the Nephilim were the offspring of "the sons of God" and "the daughters of humans," which many scholars believe means the offspring of divine (perhaps angelic) and human cohabitation (much like the Greek Titans).[18] Whatever the meaning, the result of this "unnatural" union is a race of "mighty heroes from long ago, men of renown,"[19] who, according to the spies, made grown men look like insects. No doubt, this was an exaggeration, but it had its desired effect. Turning a deaf ear to Joshua's and Caleb's admonitions to trust Yahweh and invade the land, the people begin to weep and complain in a manner that is all too familiar:

If only we had died in the land of Egypt or in this wilderness! Why is Yahweh bringing us to this land to fall by the sword? Our wives and our children will become plunder! Would it not be better for us to return to Egypt?

NUMBERS 14:2B–3

Then comes the clincher:

And they said to one another, "Let us select a leader and return to Egypt!"

NUMBERS 14:4

That's it. The people have pushed God too far. God informs Moses that he is going to destroy the Israelites and begin afresh with him, making Moses "a nation greater and mightier than they."[20] But Moses, concerned that the surrounding nations might misunderstand God's wrath as an inability to accomplish his mission of bringing the people into their Promised Land, asks Yahweh to exercise his mercy, just as he has done "from Egypt until now."[21] Yahweh agrees, but with one condition, a condition that underscores once more the significance of the number ten when counting offenses against God. Yahweh declares to Moses,

According to your word, I have pardoned them. Nevertheless, as I live, the whole earth will be filled with the glory of Yahweh, for all the people who have seen my glory and my signs that I performed in Egypt and in the wilderness, and have tested me these *ten times* and have not listened to my voice, will not see the land that I swore to their fathers; all those who have despised me will not see it.

NUMBERS 14:20–23

Yahweh has been keeping track of Israel's rebellions throughout their wilderness wanderings, and they have just reached their limit: TEN! Just as Pharaoh is given ten opportunities to change his heart and comply with Yahweh's request to "let my people go," so this generation of Israelites is given ten opportunities to change its collective heart and comply with Yahweh's commands. Both groups fail, and, as a result, God renders severe judgment upon both nations. For Egypt, the punishment is the death of its firstborn and the destruction of its army at the Red Sea. For Israel, the punishment is the death of all those who witnessed God's miracles in Egypt and the wilderness, yet still rebelled against him "these ten times."

God tells Moses that everyone twenty years of age and older will perish in the desert without seeing the fulfillment of God's promise, made long ago to their ancestors Abraham, Isaac, and Jacob.[22]

Given this pattern of "ten strikes and you're out," a pattern that we have observed shortly before and after the giving of the Ten Commandments, we should not be surprised to discover that the Ten Commandments themselves will be the basis upon which Israel will be judged as a nation. If the Israelites succeed in keeping God's commandments, they are promised blessing upon blessing in the land that God is giving them. Moses, in one of his final addresses to the people, declares,

> And it will be that if you attentively listen to the voice of Yahweh your God, to guard and to do all his commandments that I am commanding you today, Yahweh your God will set you high above all the nations of the earth, and all these blessings will come upon you and overtake you because you listened to the voice of Yahweh your God.
>
> DEUTERONOMY 28:1–2

Moses then describes blessings in everything imaginable, including productive crops, abundant livestock, numerous offspring, and protection from their enemies.[23]

However, if the Israelites break their covenant with God, then they too will be broken as a nation. Moses continues,

> But if you do not listen to the voice of Yahweh your God to keep and to do all his commandments and laws that I am commanding you today, then all these curses will come upon you and overtake you.
>
> DEUTERONOMY 28:15

The curses that Moses describes are the reverse of the blessings mentioned above, with many other disasters besides.[24] When people ask why these disasters befell Israel, Yahweh's so-called "chosen people," they will be told,

> Because they forsook the covenant of Yahweh, the God of their ancestors, which he made with them when he brought them out of the land of Egypt. Therefore, Yahweh's anger burned against that land and he brought upon it all the curses that are written in this book. Yahweh uprooted them from their land in anger and in rage and in great fury and he cast them into another land, as it is to this day.
>
> DEUTERONOMY 29:24, 26–27

Just as Adam and Eve are "exiled" from the Garden of Eden for their disobedience to God's command, and just as Cain is "exiled" from the land and the presence of God for his disobedience, so the nation of Israel will be exiled into another land for their disregard of God's commands.

What is interesting, and often overlooked, is that had the Bible not referred to these commandments as "ten words," there would probably be considerable disagreement about exactly how many commandments are represented in the lists found in Exodus 20 and Deuteronomy 5, since their division is not immediately obvious. Yet, because the Bible *does* tell us their number, different tra-

Numbering of *The Ten Commandments* Exodus 20:2–17	Jewish Tradition	Christian Traditions	
		Roman Catholic, Anglican, and Lutheran	*Orthodox and Reformed*
I am Yahweh your God who brought you out of the land of Egypt, out of the house of bondage. (EXOD. 20:2)	1	Prologue	Prologue
You shall have no other gods before me. (EXOD. 20:3)			1
You shall not make for yourself an idol, whether in the form of anything which is in the sky above, or on the earth below, or in the waters below the earth. (EXOD. 20:4) You shall not bow to them and you shall not serve them, because I Yahweh your God am a zealous God, visiting the sin of the parents upon the children, upon the third and fourth generations of those who hate me, (EXOD. 20:5) but showing lovingkindness to the thousandth (generation) of those who love me and to those who keep my commandments. (EXOD. 20:6)	2	1	2
You shall not lift up the name of Yahweh your God in vain. (EXOD. 20:7)	3	2	3
Remember the Sabbath day and keep it holy. (EXOD. 20:8) Six days you shall labor, and you shall do all your work. (EXOD. 20:9) But the seventh day is a Sabbath to Yahweh your God; you shall not do any work, you or your son or your daughter, your male servant or your female servant or your livestock or the resident alien within your gates. (EXOD. 20:10) For in six days Yahweh made the sky and the earth, the sea and all that is in them, and he rested on the seventh day.	4	3	4

Numbering of The Ten Commandments (cont.) Exodus 20:2–17	Jewish Tradition	Christian Traditions	
		Roman Catholic, Anglican, and Lutheran	Orthodox and Reformed
Therefore, Yahweh blessed the seventh day and made it holy. (EXOD. 20:11)	4	3	4
Honor your father and mother, so that your days may be lengthened in the land that Yahweh your God is giving you. (EXOD. 20:12)	5	4	5
You shall not murder. (EXOD. 20:13)	6	5	6
You shall not commit adultery. (EXOD. 20:14)	7	6	7
You shall not steal. (EXOD. 20:15)	8	7	8
You shall not bear false witness. (EXOD. 20:16)	9	8	9
You shall not covet your neighbor's house. (EXOD. 20:17)		9	
You shall not covet your neighbor's wife, or his male servant, or his female servant, or his ox, or his donkey, or anything that belongs to your neighbor.	10	10	10

ditions, whether Jewish or Christian, agree there are ten commandments. The problem, however, is that these traditions do not all agree on how to count the commandments. The chart presents the differing views.

Jewish tradition counts the statement "I am Yahweh your God who brought you out of the land of Egypt, out of the house of bondage" as the first commandment, while the other traditions begin counting the commandments with the statement "You shall have no other gods before me." Which is correct?

To help us answer this question we must place Israel's covenant with God into its ancient Near Eastern context. What we learn from the cultures that surrounded Israel is that a treaty or covenant between two parties often began with what scholars refer to as an "historical prologue." This prologue, or preamble as it is sometimes called, was intended to recount what the first (and often superior) party of the agreement had done for the second party, establishing the reasons why the second party owed allegiance to the first. Thus, with the opening statement "I am Yahweh your God who brought you out of the land of Egypt, out of the house of bondage," Yahweh sets forth the reason why Israel should worship and obey him. In essence, Yahweh argues, *"Because* I have released you from Egyptian slavery, you shall keep my commandments. Therefore, you shall have no other gods before me, you shall not make for yourselves any idols, you shall not lift up my name in vain, etc." So, while this opening statement is certainly connected with the first commandment, it is, in actuality, connected with all of them, giving the reason for Israel's allegiance to Yahweh and obedience to his commands.

Another discrepancy in numbering arises because the Jewish, Roman Catholic, Anglican, and Lutheran traditions join the injunction against making idols with the injunction to have no other gods before Yahweh, while the Orthodox and Reformed traditions count them as two separate commands.[25] As a result, the Roman Catholic, Anglican, and Lutheran traditions count this block of material as the first commandment, the Jewish tradition as the second, and the Orthodox and Reformed traditions as both commandments one and two. Consequently, the second commandment in the Roman Catholic, Anglican, and Lutheran reckoning is the third commandment in the Jewish, Orthodox, and Reformed traditions, and so on.

Therefore, when we get to the end of the commandments, what constitutes a single commandment for the Jewish, Orthodox, and Reformed traditions ("You shall not covet . . .") is divided into two commandments in the Roman Catholic, Anglican, and Lutheran traditions. This disagreement over how to count the last commandment actually highlights one of the main differences among the Ten Commandments as we have them in Exodus 20 and Deuteronomy 5. In Exodus 20, the list of items belonging to one's neighbor that should not be coveted does not exactly match the items or the order given in Deuteronomy 5. The following chart summarizes the differences.

Exodus 20:17	Deuteronomy 5:18
1. house	1. wife
2. wife	2. house
?	3. field
3. male or female servant	4. male or female servant
4. ox	5. ox
5. donkey	6. donkey
6. or anything that belongs to your neighbor	7. or anything that belongs to your neighbor

Actually, the difference in order between "house" and "wife" and the addition of the word "field" in Deuteronomy tells only half the story. There is also a difference in the verbs used to denote "coveting" in these two passages. Again, we place the texts side by side to highlight the differences.

Exodus 20:17	Deuteronomy 5:18
You shall not **covet** your neighbor's house; you shall not **covet** your neighbor's wife, or his male servant, or his female servant, or his ox, or his donkey, or anything that belongs to your neighbor.	And you shall not **covet** your neighbor's wife; and you shall not **desire** your neighbor's house, his field, or his male servant, or his female servant, his ox, or his donkey, or anything that belongs to your neighbor.

In Exodus 20, where "house" is listed first, the same verb is used twice to describe the act of "coveting" *(tachmod)*. Yet, in Deuteronomy 5, this word for coveting is used only in relation to the wife, and a different word, translated here as "desire" *(titavveh)* is attached to the other items. In reality, these two words are very close in meaning, both carrying the idea of "to desire." But in Deuteronomy there does seem to be an effort to distinguish between the act of desiring another's wife and desiring another's property, whereas in Exodus no linguistic distinction is made. Whether or not Deuteronomy reflects a more "enlightened" view regarding the status of women in the ancient world (that is, by not treating them as "property") will be addressed in a later chapter where this commandment is discussed in more detail. For now, we want only to observe that it was the presence of these two different verbs in Deuteronomy that no doubt influenced the Roman Catholic, Anglican, and Lutheran traditions to count these as two different commandments. However, in light of the evidence from Exodus where the same verb is used, as well as evidence to be discussed later, it would seem that the Jewish, Orthodox, and Reformed traditions are correct in counting the injunction against coveting as one commandment. Therefore, it is the opinion of most scholars that the proper numbering of the commandments should be as follows:

The Ten Commandments

1. You shall have no other gods before me
2. You shall not make for yourself an idol
3. You shall not lift up the name of Yahweh your God in vain
4. Observe the Sabbath day and keep it holy
5. Honor your father and your mother
6. You shall not murder
7. You shall not commit adultery
8. You shall not steal
9. You shall not give false witness
10. You shall not covet

Nine Commandments?

So far we have emphasized the significance of the number ten in our discussion of the Ten Commandments. Yet, what about the reference to nine commandments in the title of this book? Which commandment do we omit and why? While a complete answer to these questions will have to wait until the end of our journey, some initial observations are in order.

The Heart of the Matter

A closer look at the tenth commandment reveals that it is not a verifiable crime. Someone could desire another's spouse or house or oxen and never be found out until that desire is accompanied by an action. Yet, once that action is taken, then one of the other commandments comes into play. So, for example, if one covets his or her neighbor's spouse, and acts on that desire, then one has committed adultery. If one covets his or her neighbor's property, and acts on that desire, then one has stolen, and so on. What we will discover is that while the coveting addressed by the tenth commandment serves as the impetus for the violation of a number of the preceding commandments, it is never singled out as a crime by itself, that is, without an accompanying violation of one of the other commandments. Coveting is clearly the driving force behind a number of the other commandment violations in Israel's history, and discovering how this last commandment interacts with the others will give us important insight into why this injunction was believed to warrant its own place among "the Ten."

Let the Journey Begin

We are now ready to begin our journey, which will take us from the birth of a nation through its ascendancy, to its eventual decline and calamitous fall; from the bondage of slavery in a foreign land, to the courts of kings in the "Promised Land"; from the inner sanctum of the Temple in the capital city of Jerusalem, to the countryside altars of alternate worship dispersed throughout

Canaan. This will be a journey to discover the scarlet thread that runs through the history of Israel, tracing its path of disobedience and disregard for its covenant obligations embodied in the Ten Commandments, a path that will lead to exile, to Israelites becoming once again "strangers in a strange land."

The First & Second Commandments

You shall have no other gods before me

You shall not make for yourself an idol

The first two of the Ten Commandments, like many of the others, are the subject of extensive discussion and debate among scholars. The aforementioned numbering problems (is this commandment one, two, or one and two?) have only been part of the controversy.[1] Some of the most interesting discussions surround what it means to have no other gods *before* Yahweh.[2] Does this mean that other deities could be tolerated as long as Yahweh was given priority (a belief system known as henotheism)? Or, while acknowledging there are other gods, is this a demand that Israel worship *only* Yahweh (a belief system known as monolatry)? Or are we to understand this command the way it has been traditionally understood, as denying the existence of all other gods except Yahweh (a belief system known as monotheism)?

While the traditional approach is often assumed to be the correct one, cross-cultural comparisons, as well as closer scrutiny of certain biblical passages, have called this understanding into question.

Whether we look at the religions of ancient Mesopotamia, Egypt, Greece, or even Canaan, we find many gods being worshiped. Even though an individual city or nation might have its chief deity, the cultures of the ancient Near East recognized and gave homage to a wide assortment of gods and goddesses. For example, Assyria's chief deity, and the one from whom the nation

Conquered Deities. *This wall relief, showing Assyrian soldiers carrying the statues of gods taken from a captured town, was discovered at Nimrud in present-day Iraq. Often, idols from conquered nations were placed in the temple of the conquering nation's chief deity as a sign of their defeat and submission to the "superior" god or goddess. A similar action is presented to us in the Bible (1 Samuel 5). After defeating the Israelites, the Philistines take the Ark of Yahweh and place it in the temple of their chief deity, Dagon. However, in the biblical account, it is Dagon who "submits" to Yahweh, as the statue of Dagon falls face first before the Ark and its head and hands break off—a sign of impotence in the presence of the superior Yahweh. (Illustration courtesy of Z. Radovan, Jerusalem.)*

and capital derived its name, was Ashur. Nevertheless, Assyrian religion acknowledged a whole pantheon of deities and, on occasion, even incorporated new deities into their pantheon from their contact with (usually via conquest of) other nations. In light of this practice, could Yahweh be to Israel what Ashur was to Assyria—the "top god," but not the only god? And if so, did Yahweh always hold this position of priority in Israelite religion?

Did Israel Ever Have Other Gods Before Yahweh?

In a chance discovery in 1928, a Syrian farmer exposed an ancient tomb while plowing a field. What followed was the unearthing of a once bustling coastal city-state known in ancient times as Ugarit (modern Ras Shamra).[3] Within the palace complex at Ugarit there was discovered a collection of sacred writings that give us a unique look into Canaanite religion and society of the fourteen and thirteen centuries B.C.E. While we already had glimpses of Canaanite culture from descriptions in the Bible (usually in the form of condemnatory remarks), the texts from Ugarit give us the perspective of the "other guys." These texts show that although only a small number of gods play an active role in their mythologies, god-lists found at Ugarit demonstrate that literally hundreds of gods were imagined to exist. With this in view, the first of the Ten Commandments, or Decalogue, if we are to interpret it as forbidding the acknowledgment or worship of any other god except Yahweh, would certainly go against the grain of what seems normative for the Canaanite culture that surrounded Israel. Yet,

A Chance Discovery. This mythological text from Ugarit (modern-day Ras Shamra in northern Syria), which gives us valuable insight into the religion of Israel's neighbors, is just one of hundreds of texts found at this ancient Canaanite site. (Illustration courtesy of G. Tortoli/Ancient Art & Architecture Collection Ltd.)

the texts from Ugarit, while giving us greater insight into ancient Canaanite religion, might shed light on the development of ancient Israelite religion as well.

Do Gods Grow Old and Retire?

A motif found in the mythological texts at Ugarit, as well as in other mythologies of the ancient Near East, is that of the senior, retiring god, who, while maintaining his formal position of authority, is largely displaced or, in some cases, completely supplanted by a younger, more energetic and active god. For example, at Ugarit, the senior god, El, usually serves as a backdrop for the exploits of the younger Canaanite storm-god, Baal.[4] When the Canaanite pantheon is threatened by the deified Sea *(Yamm)* and later by Death *(Mot),* it is the self-asserting Baal who comes to the rescue. Similar scenarios are attested in the mythologies of ancient Mesopotamia. Both Marduk in Babylon and Ashur in Assyria gradually replace the Sumerian god Enlil as the head of the Mesopotamian pantheon. In Greece, Zeus, who, like Baal, is a storm-god, replaces the older Kronos. The reason for this "changing of the god" seems, in most cases, to be tied to changing political or social configurations within a region. For example, when a people or nation gained supremacy over another people or nation, so did their representative deity. In turn, these changes were reflected in the popular mythology. Thus, when Babylon gained control over all of Mesopotamia, Marduk became the chief hero of the Mesopotamian creation story, as well as the head of the Mesopotamian pantheon.[5]

Some scholars have suggested that a parallel phenomenon may have occurred in the development of Israelite religion, that Yahweh in Israel, like Marduk in Babylon, eventually displaced an "older" regional god, in this case, the Canaanite god El.[6] These scholars argue that while we would not expect to find a myth in the Bible explaining how Yahweh rose to eminence over an older, retiring god, since the prevailing monotheism of later (and perhaps earlier) periods would have seen to it that such a narrative

Competing Deities? El *(right), the head of the Canaanite pantheon and the father of gods and humans, receives an offering while seated upon his throne. Baal (left), the Canaanite storm god and son of Dagan (biblical Dagon), is the hero of the gods in the Ugaritic mythology. Does this mythology represent a type of divine coup? Some scholars think so. (Illustrations courtesy of the Louvre, Paris, France/Ancient Art & Architecture Collection Ltd./Bridgeman Art Library [left] and Erich Lessing/Art Resource, N.Y. [right].)*

did not make it into Israel's sacred text, there appear to be remnants in the biblical traditions that such a usurpation may have occurred.

What's in a Name?

Biblical epithets for the God of the Patriarchs include *El Elyon* (God Most High), *El Olam* (Eternal God) and *El Shaddai* (usually translated as God Almighty), among others.[7] This would be expected from a people living in Canaan, since, as we have already observed, El was the chief god of the Canaanite pantheon. Yet, this very observation requires us to reconsider the translation of the above names. "El" is usually understood, at least in nearly all translations of the Bible, as a generic name for "God." Thus, El Shaddai is rendered as "God Almighty."[8] However, the evidence from Ugarit suggests that the El of biblical tradition could be understood as a personal name for God.[9] Thus, El Shaddai could be translated as "El the Almighty." Yet, is there any evidence in the Bible that El should be understood as the personal name of a deity rather than simply the generic word for "God"? And if so, should this be understood as representing an earlier phase in Israelite religion where El was the chief deity prior to the emergence of a deity named Yahweh? Let's look at the evidence.

God's Name Change

First of all, while the name Yahweh is used throughout Genesis, a passage in Exodus seems to indicate that its occurrence in these earlier narratives is anachronistic. In Exodus 6:3, Yahweh informs Moses,

> I appeared to Abraham, Isaac, and Jacob as El Shaddai, *but by my name Yahweh I was not known to them.*

Yet, a cursory perusal of the patriarchal narratives shows that Abraham, Isaac, and Jacob all use the epithet Yahweh.[10] In what sense, then, was the name Yahweh not known to the patriarchs?

It was such a question, along with others, that led scholars to postulate that different sources were used in constructing the "five books of Moses," at least one of which preserved a tradition that the name Yahweh did not come into use in ancient Israel until the time of Moses. Adding support to this theory was the observation that when the narrative strands employing different divine names are separated, many of the so-called "doublets" (stories that are very similar to one another) separate as well. For example, there are two narratives recounting the naming of Isaac. In one, Genesis 17, the divine names used are *Elohim,* the generic name for God, and *El Shaddai.* In the other, Genesis 18, only the name *Yahweh* is used.

The narrative strand that uses the divine name *Elohim* was referred to by these early scholars as "E." Similarly, the strand that employs the divine name *Yahweh* was called "J" (from the German *Jahweh,* as the theory was largely developed in Germany). Yet, it was soon discovered that within "E" there were still more doublets and stylistic differences. Because a group of these texts seemed particularly interested in priestly matters (proper sacrifice, ritual law, etc.), it was called the "Priestly" source, or "P." What was left over retained the designation "E."[11]

Although the discovery of these sources had many stages and included the contributions of numerous scholars, the most complete and compelling presentation was given by a German scholar named Julius Wellhausen, and it is therefore sometimes referred to as the Wellhausian theory, although it is more often called the Documentary Hypothesis or the JEDP theory (D for *Deuteronomist,* an independent composition consisting of the book of Deuteronomy).[12] While the Documentary Hypothesis is not without its dissenters, it has become the prevailing model within biblical scholarship for understanding the composition of the Torah.[13]

The Worship of "Other Gods" in Ancient Israel

Regardless of whether Yahweh displaced an older and retiring El in the development of Israelite religion, that Israel worshiped more than one god is well attested in the Bible itself, even though the behavior is almost always mentioned only to condemn it. Examples of such judgments against worshiping other gods, like the following from Jeremiah, could be multiplied, quite literally, a hundred times over. In Jeremiah 11:10 Yahweh declares,

> They (the nations of Israel and Judah) have returned to the iniquities of their forefathers, who refused to listen to my words, and they have gone after other gods to serve them. The house of Israel and the house of Judah have broken my covenant that I made with their fathers.

Elsewhere in Jeremiah, Yahweh remarks disparagingly,

And where are your gods that you have made for yourself?
Let them arise if they can save you in the time of your trouble, for according to the number of your cities, so are your
gods, O Judah.

JEREMIAH 2:28

The worship of many gods was clearly part of the fabric of Israelite society.

The Worship of Goddesses

So far we have spoken mostly of male deities, but what about female deities? Were goddesses worshiped in Israel as they were
among Israel's neighbors? The answer is yes. We again turn to our
informant Jeremiah to give us a report of goddess worship in Israel, an activity that apparently extended from the home of the
commoner all the way to the halls of the royal palace.

The text we will consider records the words of those who have
unashamedly made cake offerings to a goddess known as the "queen
of heaven."[15] Their only regret, they tell Jeremiah, is that they ever
stopped! Their words reveal the extent of goddess worship in Israel:

As for the message that you [Jeremiah] have spoken to us in
the name of Yahweh, we are not going to listen to you! But
rather we will certainly carry out every word that has proceeded from our mouths, by burning sacrifices to the queen
of heaven and pouring out libations to her, just as *we our-
selves, our forefathers, our kings* and *our princes* did in the cities
of Judah and in the streets of Jerusalem; for then we had
plenty of food, and were well off, and saw no misfortune.

JEREMIAH 44:16–17

Did Yahweh Have a Wife?

Although a number of scholars identify the "queen of heaven" of
the above passage with the Mesopotamian goddess Ishtar or the

Goddess Worship in Ancient Israel. *These statuettes from Judah are probably fertility figurines (perhaps even goddesses) and constitute further evidence for the worship of female deities in ancient Israel. (Illustration courtesy of Erich Lessing/Art Resource, N.Y.)*

Canaanite goddess Astarte, her actual identity remains a mystery, and many believe her to be none other than the female deity who receives so much press in the Bible—the goddess Asherah.[16] Regardless of her identity, the presence of such a prevalent female deity in Israel raises a tantalizing question. What was the perceived relationship between Yahweh and this goddess? In Egypt, Osiris' consort was Isis, in Babylon, Marduk's consort was Zarpanitum, and at Ugarit, El's consort was Asherah. Did Yahweh have a consort?

Again, the monotheism expressed in the biblical texts would

adamantly deny this possibility. Yet, as we have seen from the book of Jeremiah, the religion extolled by the prophets was not always the religion practiced by the masses, or even the royal house. In fact, recent archaeological finds have raised whole new problems surrounding the question of Yahweh's relationship to divinities of the female sort. At Kuntillet ᶜAjrud, located between the border of the southern Negev and the Sinai peninsula, a votive inscription was found dedicated to "Yahweh of Samaria and his Asherah."[17] Should "his Asherah" be understood as the well-known Canaanite goddess or is this simply a noun referring to a shrine or cultic object (perhaps a wooden pole, as we find in the Bible)?

One difficulty with interpreting this as the goddess Asherah has to do with grammar. Proper nouns (such as Asherah) should not take possessive pronouns (in this case, "his"). However, other considerations raise the possibility that this is a reference to the goddess Asherah. If we remember that Yahweh may have been associated with the Canaanite god El, then it may not be mere coincidence that Yahweh was associated with El's consort. That is to say, if we suppose that at some point in Israelite religion El was supplanted by or incorporated into Yahweh (just as, according to the biblical record, the Canaanites were both supplanted by and incorporated into Israel), the prevalent belief may have been that Yahweh, in a sense, "got the girl." Referring to Yahweh's consort as "his Asherah" may have been necessary to distinguish her from "El's Asherah." In Mesopotamia we find that gods and goddesses could be paired with different spouses at varying times and places. For example, Ashur was paired with Mulliltu, the spouse of the "older" Mesopotamian god Enlil. In fact, Ashur became known as the "Enlil of Assyria," a title that gave him greater prestige. So one might refer to Mulliltu as both Enlil's Mulliltu and Ashur's Mulliltu. Therefore, to specify Asherah as Yahweh's by the words "his Asherah" seems quite possible and even appropriate.

Whether or not this "marriage" between Yahweh and Asherah was ever realized in the popular religion of Israel, Asherah certainly played a significant role in Israelite worship. For example,

To Yahweh of Samaria and His Asherah. *This inscription, discovered at Kuntillet ʿAjrud in the southern Negev, is a votive offering painted on a piece of pottery. It represents one of two inscriptions discovered so far that mention Yahweh and "his Asherah," raising the possibility that at least to some Israelites Asherah was Yahweh's consort. Exactly how the picture on the inscription relates to the text is still a matter of considerable debate. Some scholars believe that the larger of the two standing figures (left) is Yahweh and that the other standing figure is Asherah. (Note, however, the seemingly contradictory representation of male genitalia and female breasts—though some understand the objects between the legs of both figures to be lions' tails.) Other scholars have suggested that the woman seated and playing the lyre is Asherah and that the two standing figures are Yahweh and Baal, two deities known to be in competition for Israel's (and perhaps Asherah's) devotion (see 1 Kings 18:17–40). Still others argue that the two standing figures are representations of the Egyptian god Bes (why there are two and why Bes on an inscription mentioning Yahweh no one seems able to explain) and that the woman is just that—a woman, playing the lyre as an act of worship.*

we read in 1 Kings 15 that King Asa deposed his own mother as queen because she had built an image of Asherah. In addition, Jezebel, the Sidonian princess and wife of King Ahab, had 450 prophets of Baal and 400 prophets of Asherah in her employ.[18]

Moreover, King Manasseh, whom the Bible considers one of the worst kings in Israel's history, made an image of Asherah and did the unthinkable with it. 2 Kings 21:7 gives us the details:

> Then [Manasseh] set the carved image of Asherah that he had made in the house about which Yahweh said to David and to his son Solomon, "In this house and in Jerusalem, which I have chosen from all the tribes of Israel, I will put my name forever."

Therefore, whether or not the Israelites conceived of Yahweh and Asherah as husband and wife, King Manasseh made them to dwell together.

Although more could be said regarding the prevalence of other deities in Israel, the above discussion is sufficient to demonstrate the point—the worship of many gods and goddesses in the ancient Near East, including Israel, was pandemic, and if we interpret the first commandment as meaning Yahweh should be worshiped *alone* (a position Jeremiah certainly took), then it was a tall order indeed, and one that met with limited success.

Idolatry in the Ancient Near East and Israel

The second commandment, which forbids the making of idols, fared no better than the first. Again, with idolatry we encounter a practice that was widespread among Israel's neighbors. Texts from Egypt to Babylon describe the centrality of idols to the proper worship and service of the gods. Ceremonies were performed for the idols, with the idols, and to the idols. Idols wore clothes, jewelry, and perfume, participated in banquets, marched through the streets, visited neighboring cities, and even traveled to foreign countries (all with the help of priests, of course). In fact, we have recovered a letter from a Mitanni prince informing the king of Egypt that the goddess Ishtar rather enjoyed her last visit to the Nile and was planning to return to Egypt in the near future. While such talk may seem ridiculous to us, these gestures helped to maintain peaceful relations among world powers, much as diplomatic visits do today.

Why No Idols?

Although the reason for the commandment against idols is not specified in the Ten Commandments, other passages shed light on possible explanations. In Deuteronomy 4:15–16, Moses declares,

> Therefore, for your own sake, guard yourselves carefully, since you did not see any form on the day Yahweh spoke to you at Horeb from the midst of the fire, lest you act corruptly and make for yourselves a graven image in the form of any figure.

That is, since Yahweh did not reveal himself in some anthropomorphic (human-like) or other form, the people must also refrain from making representations of him.

Isaiah 40:18–25 gives another reason why depicting Yahweh with images is unacceptable, even nonsensical.

> And to whom can you liken God? And to what image
>   can you compare him?
>
> A craftsman casts an idol, and a smith overlays it with gold,
>   forging silver chains.
> As an offering, he chooses a special wood, wood that will
>   not rot.
> He seeks out a skillful craftsman to make an image that
>   will not teeter.
>
> Do you not know? Have you not heard?
> Has it not been declared to you from the beginning?
> Have you not understood (from) the foundations of the
>   earth?
>
> He is the one who dwells above the vault of the earth,
>   and those who dwell on [the earth] are like grasshoppers.

He is the one who stretches out the heavens like a curtain,
    and spreads them like a tent in which to dwell.
He is the one who brings princes to nothing,
    the rulers of the earth he makes as though they never
    existed.

Barely are they planted, barely are they sown,
    barely has their stem taken root in the earth,
And then he blows upon them and they dry up,
And the storm wind carries them away like straw.
Therefore, to whom will you compare me,
    that I should be likened to him? says the Holy One.

Nothing of human invention could ever be adequate to capture all that Yahweh is. The one who has made everything and sits as king over all the earth and its inhabitants could never be comprehended by the human mind, let alone constructed into an image. The logic is straightforward, especially if one adopts a monotheistic perspective: How could a mere creature ever hope to accurately represent the Creator? And, in fact, one may even argue that making images to represent the Creator is prohibited because they already exist in human form. Using language almost identical to that used to describe the building of idols, God says during creation,

> Let us make humankind in our *image,* according to our *likeness.*[19]
>
> Genesis 1:26A

God has already made images of himself . . . humans! Any attempt to make another image of God, especially from an inanimate object such as wood or metal, is to degrade both God and humankind.

Despite these injunctions against idolatry, worship of a god without a representative figure would have been nearly inconceivable to the cultures of the ancient world, which helps to explain the propensity on the part of the Israelites to make images representing the divine, such as the golden calf of the story we are about to encounter.

Aaron's Golden Calf

We now come to our first account of a covenant violation, which is found in the story of the Golden Calf. This Sunday-school favorite has been indelibly etched in our minds from the scene in Cecil B. De Mille's 1956 version of *The Ten Commandments* (although the 1923 version is quite memorable too). It is an unforgettable tale not only because of the content of the story but also because it is the quintessential example of Israel's rebellion. No sooner does Yahweh deliver the Israelites from the pursuing Egyptian army by splitting the Red Sea than they lose faith (and patience) in this God and his servant Moses, who has ascended for a second time to the top of Mount Sinai to receive further instruction from Yahweh. Not having seen or heard from either in some time, the Israelites demand that Aaron make them a god to lead them to the Promised Land. We pick up the narrative in Exodus 32 at this decisive moment:

> And the people saw that Moses delayed in coming down from the mountain, and the people gathered themselves against Aaron and said to him, "Arise! Make for us gods who will go before us, because as for this man Moses, who brought us up from the land of Egypt, we don't know what happened to him!"
>
> EXODUS 32:1

Aaron, being the uncompromising pillar of virtue that he is, takes immediate action:

> Then Aaron said to them, "Strip off the gold rings that are in the ears of your wives, your sons, and your daughters, and

bring them to me." And all the people stripped off the gold rings that were in their ears, and they brought them to Aaron. And he took them from their hand, and fashioned it with a graving tool, and made a molten calf. And they said, "These are your gods, O Israel, who brought you up out of the land of Egypt." And Aaron took note and he built an altar before it. And Aaron called and said, "A feast to Yahweh tomorrow!" And they rose up early the next day, and offered burnt offerings and brought peace offerings, and the people sat down to eat and drink, and they rose up to play.

EXODUS 32:2–6

Aaron and the people, in one fell swoop, violate commandments one and two. Yahweh had declared, "You shall not have any other gods" as well as "You shall not make for yourself an idol." The people do both.

Yet, this passage raises some interesting questions. First, why is Aaron so quick to honor the people's request to "make us gods," when he knows the commandments against worshiping other gods and making idols? Second, why after making an idol does Aaron say, "A feast to Yahweh tomorrow!"? Is this an attempt to compromise between obedience to Yahweh's commands and the people's request, or an example of religious syncretism (the merging of religious practices or beliefs), or does he sincerely believe this idol is somehow identified with Yahweh worship? Last, while burnt and peace offerings are easily understood in connection with the worship of a deity, what does it mean that the people "rose up to play"? What did they "play"? Let us address these questions in turn.

Why a Golden Calf?

The answer to the first two questions is wrapped up in the reason for Aaron's decision to make a golden calf. After all, the choice of a golden calf as an object of worship should seem peculiar to us. However, an understanding of the cultic iconography of the ancient Near East reveals that Aaron's choice was quite in keeping with the religious practices of the cultures that surrounded Israel.

The calf or bull served as a symbol of strength and virility to many ancient (and, in fact, modern) cultures. For example, in Egypt the divine Apis Bull was closely associated with the king of Egypt, and, at a later period, with Egypt's chief deity, Ptah.[20] In Mesopotamia the bull-god Sin was worshiped in prominent cities such as Ur, Harran, and Neirab.[21] This is interesting, since biblical traditions record that Israel's ancestor Abraham was from Ur and resided at Harran on his way to Canaan.[22] Furthermore, texts from Ugarit inform us that one of El's epithets was "Bull El," indicating that bull imagery was closely associated with the divine, and, in this case, with a god already shown to be connected with

Egyptian Apis Bull. Upon the death of an Apis Bull in ancient Egypt, great pains were taken both to bury it and to procure its replacement, since the success of the Pharaoh's rule and the well-being of the nation were intimately linked to this sacred beast. (Illustration courtesy of Ashmolean Museum, Oxford, U.K./Bridgeman Art Library.)

The Hazor Bull. *Bull iconography, such as this bronze bull from Hazor in northern Israel, can be found throughout the ancient Near East and sheds light on why Aaron would make a "golden calf" in response to the people's demand for "a god to lead us." (Illustration courtesy of Erich Lessing/Art Resource, N.Y.)*

Israel's past.[23] In addition, the Canaanite god Baal and other storm deities are often depicted as standing on the backs of bulls, probably to emphasize their strength and their influence over the fertility of the land.

As a final piece of evidence for the prevalence of bull imagery in the ancient Near East in general, and in Israel in particular, archaeological excavations in Syria-Palestine have turned up several bull figurines, most notably at Ugarit (northern Syria), Hazor (northern Israel), and a cultic site near Shiloh (central Israel).[24] We should not be too surprised, then, when our text says that Aaron and the Israelites made and worshiped a golden calf.

The prevalence of bull or calf iconography in the ancient Near East, including Canaan, might also explain why after seceding from

Judah, Israel's new king, Jeroboam, erected two golden calves, one at Dan and the other at Bethel, as alternate worship sites to the Temple in Jerusalem.[25] Rather than these objects of worship being an innovation, Jeroboam may have reverted back to religious traditions quite familiar to the northern tribes.[26] That even Aaron, the high priest of Israel, could declare that the nation would celebrate a "feast to Yahweh" after constructing a golden calf suggests that bull iconography was also associated with Israel's chief deity.

What Kind of Play?

This leaves us with the question, What did the Israelites rise up "to play"? The truth is, we don't know—but that it wasn't football we can be sure. Yet, while the narrative does not tell us directly, close analysis of this and other texts gives us some idea of what might have gone on at this festival.

We get our first clue about what is involved in the Israelites' "play" when Joshua reports to Moses that he hears shouts of war down in the camp.[27] Moses, having just heard from Yahweh that the people were committing idolatry, corrects Joshua's mistaken perception:

> It is not the sound of a song of triumph,
>   or the sound of a song of defeat.
> It is (merely) the sound of a song I hear.
>
> EXODUS 32:18

The structure of Moses' words emphasizes that the Israelites are singing a song devoid of real meaning, as it is directed toward an idol. Had it been a song of triumph in war, or even a dirge of defeat, then it would be an event worthy of music. And, in fact, shortly before this the Israelites *were* singing a song of triumph to Yahweh for delivering them from the Egyptians at the Red Sea— certainly an event worthy of music.[28] But this feast offers no reason to sing or celebrate; it is an insult to Yahweh, as the people ascribe to this idol the role he played in the Exodus:

And they said, "These are your gods, O Israel, who brought you out of the land of Egypt."

EXODUS 32:4

But the Israelites don't stop at just making music to this idol:

And it was as [Moses] approached the camp, he saw the calf and dancing.

EXODUS 32:19

The people danced. Again, this parallels the celebration at the Red Sea in honor of Yahweh:

For when the horse of Pharaoh with his chariotry and with his horsemen went into the sea, Yahweh made the water of the sea return over them, but the children of Israel walked on dry ground in the midst of the sea. Then Miriam, the prophetess sister of Aaron, took the timbrel in her hand, and all the women went out after her with timbrels and *with dancing*. And Miriam sang to them, "Sing to Yahweh, for he has triumphed mightily, the horse and its rider he has cast into the sea."

EXODUS 15:19–21

So, at minimum, the festival connected to the golden calf involved music and dancing. But is this all that occurred during this festival?

Biblical commentators have long thought there was more. For example, Rashi, the medieval Jewish commentator, believed that this celebration also involved sexual immorality and bloodshed. Why these two activities? Rashi based his conclusions on two other occurrences of the word "to play" *(tsiheq)* in the Hebrew Bible.

One of these narratives is found in Genesis 26 and reports an event from the life of Isaac.[29] Those familiar with the book of Genesis will recall that Isaac's father, Abraham, twice pretended that his wife, Sarah, was his sister, in order to avoid being killed by monarchs who might be captivated by her beauty, since she was "exceedingly beautiful."[30] When Isaac comes of age, he pulls the same trick with his wife, Rebekah, when they visit Abimelek, the king of the Philistines, during a famine. Remarkably, this seems to be the same Abimelek who fell for Abraham's ruse. In the Abrahamic narrative, Abimelek realizes Sarah is Abraham's wife because God comes to him in a dream and says, "Behold, you are dead on account of the woman you have taken, for she is another man's wife."[31] Fortunately for Abimelek, God gives him a reprieve, since, to paraphrase Abimelek's argument, "They lied to me, and besides, I didn't lie with her."

In the case of Isaac and Rebekah, however, Abimelek does not have the benefit of a divinely inspired dream to inform him that he had taken another man's wife. Abimelek discovers the truth one day while looking out his window:

> And [Abimelek] looked and, behold, Isaac was playing with Rebekah, his wife. And Abimelek summoned Isaac and said, "Behold, she is your wife! So why did you say, 'She is my sister'"?
>
> GENESIS 26:8B–9

Now, it does not require much thought to realize that since this type of "playing" immediately indicated to Abimelek that Isaac and Rebekah were not brother and sister but husband and wife, the verb must denote some kind of intimate, perhaps sexual, activity. Applied to the story of the golden calf, a symbol of virility, the people may have been "playing" in a similar fashion.

The idea that the worship of the golden calf involved bloodshed is derived using similar reasoning, based on a narrative of a period during the life of David. In 2 Samuel 2, David's military commander, Joab, and a number of his men meet Abner, Ishbaal's military commander, and a number of his men at a watering hole. Abner makes a proposal:

> Let the young men arise and *play* before us!
>
> 2 SAMUEL 2:14

Unfortunately for these young men, the type of "play" Abner has in mind would not prove very much fun. Twelve men from each army come forward, grab their opponents by the head, and thrust their swords into their opponents' sides. All twenty-four men die together, after which a fierce battle ensues.

Given these two examples, Rashi and others concluded that the celebration inspired by the making of the golden calf included this kind of "play." And, in fact, Cecil B. De Mille's *Ten Commandments* also presents this celebration as a raucous affair. However, whether or not this kind of "play" accompanied the festivities surrounding the worship of the golden calf, we may never know.

Two Commandments with One Golden Calf

Even if all that occurred during this festival was what is explicitly described in the text, it is worth remembering that what angers Yahweh (and Moses) is not the singing and dancing (or even the sex and violence, if these actually took place) but the idolatry. In fact, to underscore the severity of the people's offense, their idolatrous act is expressed in such a way as to immediately recall the first two commandments. Yahweh says to Moses,

> Go! Descend! For your people, whom you brought up from the land of Egypt, have corrupted themselves. They have quickly turned aside from the way that I have commanded them. They have made for themselves a molten calf, and have bowed down to it and sacrificed to it, saying, "These are your gods, O Israel, who brought you up from the land of Egypt!"
>
> EXODUS 32:7–8

Note that Yahweh's report to Moses about the people's rebellion contains vocabulary paralleling the language used in the Ten Commandments.

The commandments:
"You shall not **make for yourself** an idol . . . nor **bow** to [it]" (Exodus 20:4).

Yahweh's words:

"They have **made for themselves** a molten calf, and have **bowed down** to it" (Exodus 32:8).

Lest the reader still miss the connection between this incident and the Ten Commandments, Yahweh specifically informs Moses that "they have turned quickly from the way that *I commanded them.*"[32]

As a result of this rebellion, Yahweh tells Moses that he wants to destroy all of the people.[33] Moses, however, successfully intercedes on behalf of the people, and the nation is spared . . . temporarily. When Moses comes down from the mountain and sees the golden calf and the revelry surrounding its worship, he becomes angry and throws the tablets to the ground, the very tablets, the text is careful to remind us, that were written upon by the finger of God![34] Moses then destroys the golden calf by burning it and grinding it into fine dust, after which he scatters its remains in water and makes the people drink. Following this, Moses commands the Levites to kill all those who were accomplices in the crime, which they do with religious zeal. The next day Yahweh punishes those who had escaped the Levites' sweep through the camp, and, at last, his wrath subsides. Such are the consequences of violating their covenant obligations with their God.

It is significant that Moses, upon seeing the sin of the golden calf, throws the tablets of God down to the ground, breaking them into pieces, as this symbolically represents Israel's breaking of the commandments and, hence, the covenant with their God. With the violation of commandments one and two, Israel has begun its downward trek, a trek that will take them through each commandment, one by one, book by book, until all are "broken," resulting in their exile from the Promised Land.

The Third Commandment

You shall not lift up the name of

Yahweh your God in vain

s with the first two commandments, the meaning of the third has been the subject of considerable debate. What does it mean to "lift up the name of Yahweh in vain"? Several possibilities have been suggested.

Perhaps the most common (though probably the least likely) interpretation of this commandment is that "lifting up the name of Yahweh in vain" means using the name of God while cursing or swearing. This interpretation has resulted in the washing out of many mouths, much to the chagrin of adolescents experimenting with the outer perimeters of the English language. As we will see, however, theirs has been a comparatively lenient punishment.

A second possible meaning, and one that finds some support in other ancient Near Eastern texts, is that this commandment is a prescription against swearing by the name of God *falsely*. That is, if anyone claims to be telling the truth and invokes the name of God as proof of his or her sincerity but is actually lying, then this person is guilty of "lifting up the name of Yahweh in vain." In favor of this interpretation is the fact that the invocation of divine names as evidence of one's sincerity is well attested in the ancient world, especially in international treaties. Often these documents list numerous gods as witnesses to the agreement, and, if one of the parties to the agreement violates or breaks its stipulations, then these gods are called upon to carry out the punishments specified.

The ancients, like us, realized the difficulty of ensuring whether or not someone would tell the truth or maintain their end of a bargain. Therefore, they employed an internal check—the fear of divine retribution—to help ensure people would not violate their word.

Perhaps the best-known ancient treaty type, in fact, one that relates to the Ten Commandments directly, is the suzerain-vassal (or master-servant) treaty. Rulers of dominant or conquering nations would often make these treaties with lesser nations in order to secure the lesser nations' loyalty.[1] The greater nation agreed to protect its vassal from other foreign powers, while the vassal submitted to various conditions such as paying tribute, supplying men for military service, and providing women for the royal harem. Two scholars, George Mendenhall and Kenneth Baltzer, working independently, were the first to point out that the language and structure of these treaties paralleled the Ten Commandments, or "treaty" made at Sinai.[2] Their comparison of Hittite suzerain-vassal treaties with the Ten Commandments yielded the following similarities:

A. *Preamble, introducing the suzerain of the treaty*
"I am Yahweh your God . . ."   (Exod. 20:2A; Deut. 5:6A)

B. *Historical Prologue, describing past deeds performed for the vassal*
". . . who brought you out of the land of Egypt"
(Exod. 20:2B; Deut. 5:6B)

C. *Stipulations of the treaty*
The Ten Commandments   (Exod. 20:3–17; Deut. 5:7–21)

D. *Provisions for the keeping and periodic reading of the treaty*
In the Ark of the Covenant   (Exod. 25:16; Deut. 31:9–13)

E. *Blessings and curses for treaty violations*
The blessings and curses of Moses' last sermon   (Deut. 27–28)

Like these ancient treaties, our current legal system has tried various ways of ensuring honesty when giving testimony, such as having people place themselves under oath and promise to "tell the truth, the whole truth, and nothing but the truth, so help me God." The implication of such a statement is that if the individual lies, then God will punish them. As in ancient times, however, this tactic meets with only limited success.

There is yet a third possible interpretation of "lifting up the name of Yahweh in vain," which, in many ways, is simply a more general application of the commandment as a whole. This last view understands the commandment to refer to any use of God's name for common or profane purposes, including cursing, lying, or in association with anything deemed unworthy of the divine name. Thus, a joke of questionable moral character, or perhaps of any character, that includes the name of God, would fall into this category. The goal of the commandment, then, was to prevent people from using the name of God inappropriately in *any* context.

What's in a Name?

The fear of violating this commandment led to the disuse of the divine name altogether, a custom that continues to this day among certain pious Jews. However, this is not only a modern convention. Already in the Hebrew Bible the divine name is excluded in passages where it might be impugned by its presence (a practice we believe is reflected in the story soon to be discussed). Although we do not know exactly when this practice began, we do know that at some point when those reading the Bible came to the Tetragrammaton, that is, the four *(tetra)* letters *(grammaton)* spelling the name of Yahweh (YHWH), they would say, *adonay,* a Hebrew word usually translated as "Lord" and used only when referring to Yahweh. Similarly, most English Bibles render the divine name "Yahweh" by the more impersonal title LORD (small capital letters). When the "real" word for Lord *(adonay)* appears in the Hebrew, most English Bibles translate it as "Lord" (spelled with only the first letter capitalized). Yet, sometimes Yahweh and *adonay* occur side by side, which, if these translations were to be consistent, would result in the awkward LORD Lord. In these cases, most translators render *adonay* simply as "God." Therefore, the combination "YHWH *adonay*" is translated as "LORD God." This generates some confusion, since the combination "LORD God" (Yahweh plus the actual word for God—*elohim)* also occurs in the Hebrew Bible. As a result, English readers of the Bible do not know which word is being translated as "God"—*adonay* or *elohim*. While this may seem trivial to some, as we saw in the previous chapter, the fine distinctions between the names used to refer to the deity led to one of the most influential theories of biblical scholarship—the Documentary Hypothesis.³ Thus, it behooves the careful student of the Bible to know "what's in a name."

Jehovah or Yahweh?

Many translations of the Bible render God's name as Jehovah, while in scholarly writing one often encounters the name Yahweh. Which one is correct? How did this confusion arise? The answers to these questions reveal what is an accident of history, or, if you will, a case of mistaken identity.

As we noted above, in order to avoid pronouncing the divine name, the word *adonay* was substituted when reading the text. When biblical scribes inserted vowel letters into the consonantal Hebrew text (not until near the end of the first millennium C.E.), they wrote the vowels of *adonay (a-o-a)* upon the consonants of the divine name (YHWH) resulting in Y*a*Ho*W*aH. Thus, when a cantor or reader came to the divine name in the text, these vowels served as a reminder not to pronounce the actual name of God, but to say "adonay." When those not familiar with this tradition came upon the divine name, they took the vowel letters to be the actual vowels of the divine name. Because the first *a* is shortened in Hebrew to what is rendered as an *e* in English, and the *w* is pronounced like English *v*, the result was the name Yehovah, or Jehovah in German, which carried over into English.

Yet, this is not the only misunderstanding over the proper pronunciation of the divine name that has occurred over the centuries. Some Greek translations of the Bible sought to preserve the actual Hebrew letters of the divine name, no doubt because it was believed that the written name was itself sacred.[4] Therefore, in the middle of a Greek translation of the Bible one would encounter the Hebrew characters יהוה. This worked out fine until a scribe, not aware that these were Hebrew characters, wrote down the graphically similar Greek letters ΠΙΠΙ, which changed the divine name from Yahweh to PIPI. The translation of the Bible using this name is known as the "Pipi" Bible. Who says things are lost in translation?

Leviticus: The Misunderstood Book

We now move to the narrative in Leviticus that involves the breaking of the third commandment. Leviticus is arguably one of the most misunderstood books in the Hebrew Bible. Not that interpretation of the book raises any particular problems more difficult than in any other book—in fact, Leviticus is often the first book students of Hebrew study, since the Hebrew is exceptionally "orthodox." The problem is that most people have neither the patience nor the stomach to read through numerous laws regarding different kinds of sacrifice, what to do with the blood, what to do if mildew breaks out in a house, or what to do if a wound has a certain color discharge. Of course, many of us do not have the patience or stomach for medical books that describe matters equally unsettling, but we are glad that there are people who do, especially when we are in need of medical attention. While the analogy is not exact, ancient Israelites would not have had the same aversion toward the Book of Leviticus that many modern readers do, and, although the things covered in the book seem far from our realm of experience, they were of practical importance to the running of the Levitical sacrificial calendar, and provided as well for a basic medical guide for dealing with some common ailments or health hazards.[5]

Because of the abundant lists of laws and procedures in the

Book of Leviticus, one is surprised to find any narrative at all, which underscores the significance of the story about to be discussed.

In the Book of Leviticus a seemingly endless list of laws is interrupted by a story of an unnamed violator of one of the Ten Commandments—and not just any commandment, but the third commandment, and this in the third book of the Bible. This sequence of violations does not seem to be accidental, especially since a list of laws in the next book, the Book of Numbers, is also interrupted to tell the story of an unnamed violator of the fourth commandment.[6] In fact, these stories are so similar that they beg for explanation and comparison. But first things first—the narrative involving the third commandment.

Blasphemy

We encounter our episode of blasphemy in Leviticus 24, immediately following various laws on the preparation of bread for the golden table within the Tabernacle. In this context, our story sticks out like a sore thumb:

And the son of an Israelite woman [his father was an Egyptian] went out into the midst of the people of Israel, and the son of the Israelite woman and an Israelite man contended with one another in the camp. And the son of the Israelite woman blasphemed the Name, and cursed. And they brought him to Moses. [His mother's name was Shelomit, the daughter of Dibri, of the tribe of Dan.] And they placed him into custody until Yahweh's decision should be made known to them. And Yahweh said to Moses, "Take the one who cursed outside of the camp, and let all the ones who heard him lay their hands upon his head, and let all the congregation stone him. And to the people of Israel you shall say, 'Anyone who curses his God shall bear his sin, and the one who blasphemes the name of Yahweh shall be put to death.' All the congregation shall certainly stone him; as with the sojourner so with the native, when he blasphemes the Name, he shall be put to death."

LEVITICUS 24:10–17

We should notice first that when the unnamed man is said to have blasphemed God, God's actual name is replaced by "the Name" *(hashem* in Hebrew). This is the first, and perhaps only, situation where this alternate name for God is used in the Bible.[7] Moreover, this use would appear to be a clear case of the practice mentioned above—the omission of the divine name where "the Name" may be compromised by its presence. That is, the concern to avoid misusing the divine name exists even when reporting its misuse by someone else!

Another example of protecting the divine name in a compromising context is found in the Book of Job. But in this case the word that is changed is not God's name, but what someone suggests doing to God. Those familiar with the story will remember Job's wife and her pointed advice after all of Job's hardships: "Curse God and die!"[8] What is interesting, and not apparent in most English translations, is that this is not what the text really says. In Hebrew, Job's wife literally exclaims, *"Bless* God and die!" This does not seem like such bad advice (except, perhaps, the second part). On what basis, then, do most English translators believe the author meant "curse"?

That Job's wife advised him to curse God is apparent from both the immediate context and the surrounding material. In relation to the immediate context, Job exclaims in response to his wife's advice, "You speak like one of the foolish would speak! Shall we receive good from God, and not receive evil?" The narrator adds, "In all this Job did not sin with his lips."[9] Therefore, that Job's wife intended him to curse God, and not bless him, seems apparent. There is yet other evidence, coming from earlier in the book, that the word *bless* should be rendered as *curse.*

In chapter 1 we are told that Job regularly offered sacrifices on behalf of his children, "for Job said, 'Perhaps my sons have sinned and *cursed* God in their hearts.' "[10] Again, the word translated as "cursed" is, in fact, "blessed," but it would make little sense if Job was concerned about his sons *blessing* God. The author of Job, or perhaps a later copyist, could not bring himself to write the word "curse" in reference to God, even when recounting the words of another, so deep did the fear of breaking the third commandment run.

Returning to our narrative, we have already observed that the violator is unnamed, making the story somewhat surreal and didactic: through the disobedience of this anonymous man, precedent is set for any future violations of this commandment. While we are not given the man's name, we are given his parentage: he is the son of an Egyptian father and Israelite mother.[11] What the significance is of specifying his parentage cannot be stated with certainty. However, there are at least a couple of possibilities. Perhaps it would be more understandable that the blaspheming of Israel's God would be done by someone of mixed parentage, and therefore possibly of mixed devotion to that God. After all, according to Israelite tradition, Yahweh was the cause of numerous injuries to the Egyptians and their gods.[12] Therefore, it is not hard to imagine that in a conflict with an Israelite, one who might have felt somewhat of an outsider would resort to badmouthing the other's deity, a sort of "my god is bigger than your god" defense. Another possible reason for mentioning this man's mixed parentage is to add force to Yahweh's injunction that the law of blasphemy, in fact, all of the Ten Commandments, pertains to both "the native Israelite and the non-native."[13] This incident, then, is a perfect test case as to the applicability of this law.

We are also told that this commandment violation occurred as two men were "contending one with another."[14] We have purposely used the ambiguous phrase "contend with," since the Hebrew root used in this narrative *(natsah)* can be rendered either as a verbal bout (as in the RSV translation "[they] quarreled") or as an actual physical fight (as most other translations seem to understand it, including the NIV "a fight broke out," the NASB "[they] struggled with each other," and the KJV "[they] strove together"). The Septuagint, or Greek translation of the Hebrew Bible, uses a word that is equally ambiguous, *maxomai,* which can mean either to quarrel or to struggle, though the latter is more prevalent. That this conflict had a verbal element is clear, since this is what all the fuss is about. It involved the fatal use of words, cursing God. But did these two men come to blows as well?

While both "to quarrel" and "to fight" are attested meanings of Hebrew *natsah,* the particular verb form we encounter in this passage (known as the "Niphal") involves some form of physical altercation in all other occurrences. To demonstrate this point, a couple of examples will suffice.

Moses' Temper

Anyone familiar with Moses' nonillustrious rise to leadership re-members his attempt to seek revenge for an Egyptian taskmaster's abusive treatment of an Israelite slave.[15] After making sure no one was looking, Moses strikes the taskmaster and kills him, then buries him in the sand. So far our verbal root has not occurred. However, the next day Moses sees two Hebrews contending (the Niphal of *natsah)* with one another.[16] Moses' words of interven-tion, though ineffective, illuminate the meaning of our word. Moses asks the aggressor, "Why did you *strike* your fellow He-brew?"[17] Here, the word for strike *(nakah)* is explicit, for this is the same thing Moses saw the Egyptian taskmaster doing to the He-brew slave the day before, and it is what Moses did to the Egyp-tian in response, resulting in the taskmaster's death. Thus, here, *natsah* seems to involve a physical skirmish.

Sibling Rivalry

Another story that gives us insight into the meaning of the word *natsah* recounts an event from the life of David. In 2 Samuel 14 a widow comes before David to beg for the life of her one remain-ing son, even though this son has killed his brother. Unbeknownst to David, the whole account is actually a ruse orchestrated by his general, Joab, to persuade David to end the banishment of his son, Absalom, who was being punished for murdering his half-brother, Amnon.[18] The ruse works, and David allows Absalom to return to Jerusalem. However, what concerns us here is the woman's description of the fratricide and the light it sheds on the meaning of our word. The woman explains,

> Your maidservant had two sons, and the two of them contended *(natsah)* with one another in the field, and there was no deliverer between them, so one struck *(nakah)* the other and killed him.
>
> 2 SAMUEL 14:6

Again, this narrative makes it plain that *natsah* includes or is accompanied by a physical struggle, for again it uses the word for "to strike," *nakah,* to describe this altercation. The Niphal of *natsah* in our narrative should thus most likely be understood as involving a physical assault.

The Judicial Process

Despite the physical altercation between the Israelite man and the man of mixed parentage, the encounter included a most inappropriate (and fatal) use of words.[19] Thus, what began as a conflict between two individuals soon became the business of the whole community. The people who heard the man curse God during this fight brought him to Moses in order to obtain a ruling from Yahweh about what should be done, since no punishment is attached to the injunction against blasphemy as it is given in the Ten Commandments. The penalty is then communicated to Moses by Yahweh—death by stoning. Moreover, the whole community is to participate in the punishment in order to exonerate all of Israel from the guilt of this one person's disobedience. This pattern of punishment communicated by Yahweh will come up again with other command violations. In fact, a similar penalty was exercised in our first narrative about the golden calf. The Levites were instructed by God (via Moses) to go through the camp and kill all of those who were guilty.[20] Any guilty party escaping this first punishment was later punished by Yahweh himself. Thus, in both cases, the whole community is purged of the guilt brought upon it by the violations.

As mentioned above, the present narrative is independent of its immediate context, suggesting that it could have been placed anywhere in the Pentateuch (during the life of Moses). That it is placed here, amidst laws wholly unrelated to it and in a book not given to narrative, hints that something is up. Commandment number three has been broken in book three. If this unusual story in an unusual context has raised our suspicions that someone is attempting to make a point about Israel's covenant unfaithfulness as it relates to the Ten Commandments, then the next narrative, showing the breaking of the fourth commandment in the fourth book of the Bible, will confirm those suspicions.

The Fourth Commandment

Remember the Sabbath day and keep it holy

he fourth commandment pertains to the Sabbath day, the one day of each week on which an individual is to cease from work. The reason given for observing this statute goes back to Creation itself:

> For six days Yahweh made the heavens and the earth, the sea, and all that is in them, and he rested the seventh day. Therefore Yahweh blessed the Sabbath day, and made it holy.
>
> EXODUS 20:11

Thus, the faithful Israelite must rest on the Sabbath, just as God rested on the seventh day of his work of Creation. In this way, humans can participate in the *imago Dei,* the "image of God."

However, many have noted that in the second imparting of the Law in Deuteronomy a slightly different reason is given for keeping the Sabbath. Israel's observance of this commandment is connected to another great act of Yahweh—the redemption of Israel from Egypt:

> And you shall remember that you were a servant in the land of Egypt, and that Yahweh your God brought you out from there with a mighty hand and with an outstretched arm. Therefore, Yahweh your God has commanded you to keep the Sabbath day.
>
> DEUTERONOMY 5:15

Whether the writer of Deuteronomy had a different tradition of why Israel kept the Sabbath, or whether he was seeking to explain why this command applies also to servants (because Israel was once servants of the Pharaoh and cried out for rest), or whether this is simply a reassignment of the significance of the Sabbath to the Exodus is a subject of continuing scholarly debate.[1] What is clear, though, is that the Sabbath was so central to Israel's life that it could be connected to two such great events as the Creation of the Cosmos and the Exodus from Egypt.

Yet, this still leaves unanswered several questions. What does it mean not to "work" on the Sabbath? What is work? What constitutes a violation of this commandment? Certainly plowing or harvesting one's field would be considered work. But what of the more mundane daily tasks? Making a meal? Putting on clothes? Drawing water? The text does not specify the exact parameters of this commandment, a fact that has led to quite an interpretative history as to what this injunction might mean.

The Dead Sea Scrolls and the Sabbath

However, with the discovery of the Dead Sea Scrolls and, in particular, the Damascus Document (dating to around 100 B.C.E.), we have been given a unique glimpse into later interpretations of what it meant to work on the Sabbath.[2] These include preparing food, walking over one thousand cubits beyond the limits of one's city, opening sealed vessels, assisting an animal in birthing, carrying a child while walking or, one made famous by the Gospel accounts, assisting a beast that has fallen into a pit (which we will discuss below).[3] Sexual intercourse within Jerusalem also seems to have been prohibited on the Sabbath (although this particular prohibition in the Damascus Document may refer to abstaining from sex in Jerusalem *at any time!*).

Israel's devotion to the Sabbath command is reflected in the many traditions of enemy armies attacking on this day when they knew Israel would give no resistance. The Chronicles of the Babylonian Kings record that it was on the "second day of the

Another Chance Discovery. *In 1947 a young shepherd was tending his flock near the Dead Sea when he threw a rock in an attempt to corral one of his straying sheep. What he heard—the breaking of a ceramic pot—changed the study of the Bible forever. His errant throw had entered a cave containing a cache of two thousand-year-old scrolls of the Bible and other documents. A total of eleven caves, numerous biblical scrolls, and thousands of fragments of biblical texts and other writings were discovered in subsequent years and the study of these ancient texts continues to the present day. (Illustration courtesy of Erich Lessing/Art Resource, N.Y.)*

month of Adar [March 16, 597 B.C.E.]" that Nebuchadnezzar and his troops attacked Jerusalem, a day calculated to be on a Sabbath.[4] The fall of Jerusalem is also believed to have occurred on a Sabbath, based on Babylonian and biblical records.[5] By the Maccabaean period (mid-second century B.C.E.) we find the Jews having to make the difficult decision whether to defend themselves on the Sabbath or else face utter defeat.[6]

Jesus and the Sabbath

The teachings of Jesus also reflect a concern for the Sabbath, but his concern is purportedly different from that of the Qumranic and Rabbinic teachings of his time. The Gospel of Matthew records that after Jesus healed a man on the Sabbath, he sensed the displeasure this caused among the teachers of the Law and asked, "Would not anyone lift their ox from a pit if it fell in on the Sabbath?"[7] Apparently not, at least according to the Damascus Document.[8]

Rabbinic *halakah,* or religious instruction, also tended to be quite elaborate in its teachings regarding the Sabbath in an attempt to protect it from being profaned. In fact, because of the proximity of the Sabbath command in the biblical account (Exodus 20:8–11) to the building of the Tabernacle (Exodus 25–31, specifically Exodous 31:12–17), the rabbis used the activities for constructing the Tabernacle as their basis for determining what constituted "work." As a result, they created thirty-nine classifications of activities that could not be performed on the Sabbath. These and other restrictions became so numerous that the *Mishnah,* or Jewish law, describes them as "mountains hanging on a thread"—the "thread" being the single command to rest on the Sabbath.[9]

However, among the rabbinic teachings we do find opinions similar to those of Jesus. For example, in the Gospel of John we read of a confrontation between Jesus and a crowd gathered in Jerusalem for a certain festival. Apparently Jesus knows that they are still offended by his act of healing a man on the Sabbath, so he addresses them concerning this issue:

> I did one deed, and you all are surprised at it. Moses gave you circumcision [not that it originated from Moses, but from the fathers], and on the Sabbath you circumcise a man. If a man receives circumcision on the Sabbath that the Law of Moses may not be broken, are you angry with me because I made a man's whole body well on the Sabbath?
>
> JOHN 7:21–23

The issue was that God had commanded the forefathers to circumcise all male children on the eighth day after birth. Yet, if the eighth day falls on a Sabbath, which law takes precedence: the Sabbath rest or circumcision? The religious teachers had decided that circumcision should take priority. (Childbirth also took priority over the Sabbath command, though it certainly is "work." However, a midwife could not assist with a childbirth on the Sabbath unless there was a threat to the mother's or child's life. So noteworthy was a Sabbath birth that some children born on this day even seem to have been named after the Sabbath.)[10] Jesus, using the priority of circumcision over the Sabbath as a legal precedent, argues that certainly healing someone's whole body on the Sabbath also takes priority. In fact, a saying attributed to a rabbi who was a near contemporary of Jesus suggests that a similar sentiment was felt by others within the Jewish community. Rabbi Eleazar ben Azariah said regarding the Sabbath:

> If circumcision, which affects only one of a person's limbs, takes precedence over the Sabbath, how much more should the whole of the body.
>
> *Mekhilta, Tractate Shabbata* ON EXODUS 31:12ff.

The similarities between Eleazar's and Jesus' perspectives on the Sabbath are obvious. Yet the very need to express such ideas shows that there was considerable disagreement within the Jewish community over this issue. And the Gospel's presentation of Jesus' opponents, as well as the content of other rabbinic teachings on the Sabbath, suggests that Eleazar and Jesus may have been in the minority. But they were not alone. In fact, one of Jesus' most famous sayings regarding the Sabbath is also reflected in the teachings of the rabbis.

The Sabbath Was Made for Humankind, Not Humankind for the Sabbath

One Sabbath Jesus and his disciples were walking through a grainfield. The disciples, presumably hungry, began picking some grain and eating it. Offended by this, the Pharisees questioned Jesus as to why his disciples were profaning the Sabbath. Jesus, again citing precedent (this time by analogy), answered:

> Have you not read what David did when he was in need and became hungry, he and those accompanying him? How he entered into the house of God when Abiathar was high priest, and how he ate the sacred bread, which is not lawful for anyone to eat but the priests, and how he also gave it to those who were with him?
>
> MARK 2:25–26

David and his followers transgressed the law when they were in need. Therefore, so may others transgress the law when they are in need.

Jesus follows this example with what he believes to be the essence of the Sabbath command:

> For the Sabbath was made for humankind, and not humankind for the Sabbath.
>
> MARK 2:27

In other words, God gave the Sabbath command to *benefit* humankind, not to *burden* it. Many of the religious leaders during Jesus' time seem to have lost sight of this and made observing the Sabbath a cumbersome affair—the "mountains hanging on a thread" mentioned earlier.

Yet, again, Jesus' teachings are echoed in the rabbinic sources. Rabbi Shimon ben Menasia is quoted as saying: The Sabbath was handed to you, not you to the Sabbath. Given the similarities between the teaching of Jesus and these rabbis regarding the Sabbath, the question becomes: Who influenced whom? This is an issue that continues to be debated among scholars, and any definite answers seem beyond our reach.[11] The main difficulty in answering this question is that while Jesus lived prior to these particular rabbis, we cannot automatically assume that he was the originator of these ideas. It is possible that they already could be found within the Jewish community, since their attribution to a particular rabbi may or may not reflect their actual origin. It is also possible that similar ideas could arise independently. After all, both the rabbis and Jesus had as their source the Hebrew Bible, and the priority of following the intent of the law over the letter of the law can be found in its pages (as in the above case of David and his men eating the holy bread). So who influenced whom is not as important as noting that even within the Jewish community there was a great diversity of opinion, which contributed to the richness of its life and culture, yet which also contributed to its internal strife and division.

Of Sticks and Stones

Having introduced some of the repercussions of the ambiguity of this commandment, we may better understand why in the first recorded Sabbath violation we find some confusion among the Israelites. As with the previous violation of "lifting up the name of Yahweh in vain," we are somewhat surprised by the placement of this story among various and sundry laws, suggesting that a compiler of the Bible had a choice as to where the story would go.[12] Furthermore, we are struck again by the fact that the guilty party is unnamed.[13] Other similarities with the previous narrative will become immediately obvious.

> And the people of Israel were in the wilderness, and they found a man gathering wood on the Sabbath day. And those who had found him gathering sticks brought him to Moses and Aaron and the whole congregation. And they placed him in custody, because it had not been specified what should be done to him. And Yahweh said to Moses, "The man shall be put to death, the whole congregation shall stone him with stones outside the camp." And the whole congregation brought him outside the camp, and stoned him to death with stones, as Yahweh commanded Moses.
>
> NUMBERS 15:32–36

In both Leviticus 24 and here, a violation of one of the Ten Commandments is recorded and the man responsible is arrested pending sentencing and the imposition of the appropriate punishment. In both cases, the determination of the penalty (death by stoning by the whole assembly) is made by Yahweh through direct communication with Moses. The action by God is taken to supplement the Decalogue itself, which lists the injunctions but does not specify the punishment. And the severity of the penalty serves to emphasize the centrality of these terms of the covenant. Anything less than the removal of the offender would implicate the whole community in the offense and ultimately lead to the abrogation of the compact and the dissolution of the nation.

Editorial Intent

Thus, we have seen the fourth commandment broken in the fourth book of the Bible, and in a context that suggests an editor or author deliberately placed it there. But for what purpose? Again, that the narratives recounting the violations of the third and fourth commandments in the third and fourth books of the Bible would be so similar in content and structure, and that both are clearly "out of place," strongly suggests that literary and theological purposes are at work—purposes that sought to demonstrate to a community in exile that their present situation was their own doing, the result of their complete violation of the terms of the covenant with their God. Hence, our suspicions at the end of the last chapter seem to be confirmed. The editor has shown us his hand. However, who this editor might be and how he plays out the rest of his hand for the remaining six commandments is yet to be seen.

The Fifth Commandment

Honor your father and mother

The fifth commandment marks the transition from laws concerning Israel's interaction with their God to laws concerning their interaction with one another. Yet, this shift is fitting, since the violation of the fifth commandment occurs in a book full of transitions.

Transitions

One such transition is Moses' impending death. Due to his sin at Meribah, which we will explore in a moment, Moses is destined to die without entering the Promised Land. Therefore, in order to remind the Israelites of God's commitment to them and their commitment to God, Moses delivers a series of speeches recounting God's faithfulness toward Israel and their covenant obligations toward God. This restatement of the law has given rise to this book's name: Deuteronomy, a word meaning "second" (Greek: *deutero*) "law" (Greek: *nomos*). (The Hebrew name, *Devarim*, or "words," as with the other books of the Torah, comes from the first word or words of the book; in this case, "These are the words that Moses spoke . . .")

Another major transition about to take place is the people's entry into and dispersion throughout the land. After the book of Joshua, gone will be the days when a commandment violator is brought to a central leader (i.e., Moses or Joshua), who then consults God as to the appropriate punishment for the crime and participates in its enforcement. Soon the elders of individual cities will determine and carry out the punishment for commandment violations.

These transitions will also have an effect on the form of our next violation. Whereas the previous covenant violations had an accompanying narrative, Deuteronomy presents the breaking of the fifth commandment as case law in a speech by Moses. Yet, that this particular incident is to be connected with the previous two will become evident upon a close analysis of the text. Before such an analysis, however, we need to ask what it means to "honor your father and mother."

A "Weighty" Command

The word translated in most English translations as "honor" comes from the Hebrew root *kabed,* which means "to be heavy." This word appears throughout the Hebrew Bible, though it is obscured in most of its occurrences because of translation. A few examples should suffice to give us a sense of the breadth of its use.

After Abraham settles in Canaan, a severe famine comes upon the land, forcing him to sojourn to Egypt in search of food. A similar famine occurs during the life of Isaac, though he is commanded not to go to Egypt to find relief. In both of these cases, the word used to describe the famine as "severe" is actually our word "heavy." Thus, a translation that conveys more the literal sense of the original Hebrew, and yet still makes perfect sense, is "And the famine was *heavy* upon the land."

Other examples obscured by translation include the following:

And Abram was very rich [literally, "very heavy"] in cattle, in silver and in gold.

GENESIS 13:2

And they (Jacob's sons and the Egyptians) went as far as the threshing floor of 'Atad, which is across the Jordan, and they lamented there with a very great and sorrowful [literally, "a very big and heavy"] lamentation.

GENESIS 50:10

And Yahweh said to Moses, "Pharaoh's heart is hardened [literally, "is heavy"], he refuses to let the people go."

EXODUS 7:14

Of course, this root is not without its literal uses as well, although examples are far fewer:

And as he [a messenger] mentioned the Ark of God, Eli fell backward from upon his seat by the side of the gate and his neck was broken and he died, for he was an old man, and *heavy.*

1 SAMUEL 4:18

And when he [Absalom] cut his hair—and it was at the end of every year he would cut it, because it was *heavy* upon him and he would cut it—he weighed the hair of his head, two hundred shekels according to the king's weight.

2 SAMUEL 14:26

God's "Weightiness"

One final example of the Hebrew root *kabad* will shed further light on the meaning of "honoring your father and mother." It is found in the word used to express God's presence among his people or his "glory," as it is usually translated. The Hebrew word translated in English as "glory" is *kabod,* which might be understood as God's "heaviness" or "weightiness," that is, his importance or his significance. Thus, when Moses ascends Mount Sinai to receive the law, "The glory (*kabod*) of Yahweh settled on Mount Sinai, and the cloud covered it for six days, and on the seventh day he called to Moses from the midst of the cloud,"[1] and upon completion of the construction of the Tabernacle, "the cloud covered the Tent of Meeting, and the glory (*kabod*) of Yahweh filled the Tabernacle. And Moses was unable to enter the Tent of Meeting, because the cloud dwelt upon it, and the glory (*kabod*) of Yahweh filled the Tabernacle."[2]

Did Moses Have Horns?

In fact, it is Yahweh's glory, his *kabod,* that causes Moses' face to become so noticeably altered that the people cannot bear to look at him. We pick up the narrative after Moses has spent forty days on the mountain exposed to God's glory.

> And it was as Moses descended from Mount Sinai—and the two tablets of the testimony were in the hand of Moses as he descended from the mountain—Moses did not know that the skin of his face was radiant because he had been speaking with [God]. And Aaron and all the people of Israel saw Moses, and behold, the skin of his face was radiant, and they were afraid to come near him.
>
> EXODUS 34:29–30

The question that comes out of this text is whether or not we should understand Moses' altered appearance as "radiant" (as most English translations of the Bible do) or as something else, since the Hebrew word rendered here as "radiant" is also the word for "horned."[3] Thus, Michelangelo, in his famous sculpture of Moses, represents him as having two horns on his head.[4] Yet, because the passage describes Moses' whole face as being affected by this encounter, one scholar, William H. C. Propp of the University of California at San Diego, has suggested that Moses' face may not have become bright, but disfigured (covered by hornlike wounds or bumps, perhaps blisters) by the intensity of God's presence.[5] If this is the case, then the reason that the Israelites could not bear to look at Moses' face was not because of the brilliance of its appearance, but because of the severity of its wounds.

Moses' Mistake

One of Deuteronomy's transitions is Moses' death, one of the most heartrending moments in all the Bible. Beneath the relative calm of the narrative flows an undercurrent of deep emotive power.

Moses' Horns. *This sculpture by Michelangelo shows Moses with horns. It was common in medieval and Renaissance art to portray Moses with horns, since the Hebrew word often rendered as "radiant" can also mean "horned" (Exodus 34:29). One scholar has even suggested that Moses' face was blistered or disfigured as a result of being in the divine presence. That is, rather than Moses' radiance causing the people to fear, it may have been his appearance that caused such dread. (Illustration courtesy of San Pietro in Vincoli, Rome. Italy/SuperStock.)*

And Moses went up from the plains of Moab to Mount Nebo, to the top of Pisgah, which is opposite Jericho. And Yahweh showed him all the land, Gilead as far as Dan . . . And Yahweh said to him, "This is the land that I swore to Abraham, to Isaac and to Jacob, saying, 'To your offspring I will give it.' I have allowed you to see it with your eyes, but you will not cross over to there." And Moses, the servant of Yahweh, died there in the land of Moab according to the word of Yahweh. And he [Yahweh?] buried him in the valley in the land of Moab, opposite Beth-Peor, and no one knows his burial place to this day.

DEUTERONOMY 34:1, 4–5

Why, after all that Moses had done to lead the rebellious Israelites out of slavery in Egypt, is he allowed only to see the land, but not enter it? What offense could be so grave as to bar Moses from finally reaching his goal? The answer to these questions will help us understand the importance of giving honor to those to whom it is due.

Aaron's Errant Sons

In order to place Moses' sin into its proper context, we must go back to an enigmatic story recounting the death of two of Aaron's sons. In Exodus 30:9, God specifically commands the Israelite priests not to offer him "foreign incense." This prohibition seems to be aimed at forbidding the incorporation of foreign cultic practices into the worship of Yahweh. Thus, "foreign" or "strange" (as some translations render it) incense would mean an offering not specifically commanded by Yahweh, and which is probably borrowed from the nations surrounding Israel. That Israel *did* incorporate such foreign practices, and even foreign deities, into its worship is well attested throughout the later history of Israel, and is given as one of the main causes for Israel's destruction at the hands of the Babylonians in 587/6 B.C.E. Yet, the first violation of this commandment occurs not long after it is given.

One day two of Aaron's sons enter the Tabernacle to make

their daily offerings. However, due to their impropriety, on this day they would, in essence, become the offerings.

> And the sons of Aaron, Nadab and Abihu, each took his censer and put fire in them and placed incense upon them. And they offered before Yahweh a foreign fire, which he had not commanded them. And fire came out from before Yahweh and consumed them and they died before Yahweh.
>
> LEVITICUS 10:1–2

What happens next is somewhat strange, but it is meant to communicate the severity of not honoring Yahweh by obeying his commands.

Moses, instead of expressing sympathy and sorrow over the deaths of Aaron's sons (though Moses may have felt both), communicates to Aaron why God has dealt so harshly with them:

> I [Yahweh] will show myself holy [Hebrew root: *qadash*] among those near to me, and before all the people I will be honored [Hebrew root: *kabad*].
>
> LEVITICUS 10:3

Aaron's response (or, more precisely, lack thereof) is telling:

"And Aaron was silent."

Aaron has nothing to say. Whether this is a case of "silence is golden" or an example of "if you don't have anything nice to say, don't say anything" we cannot tell. Perhaps Aaron is still in shock over the loss of his sons. Whatever the case, Moses' words and the silence of Aaron are meant to communicate the seriousness of this cultic violation.

Then, as if the deaths of his two sons were not enough, God, via Moses, tells Aaron and his two remaining sons that they may not participate in the mourning for their deaths, "lest you die and lest [Yahweh] becomes angry at the whole congregation."[6]

Aaron's sons did not honor God before the people and therefore they will not be honored.

With this background, we are now in a better position to understand the circumstances of Moses' sin and its consequences.

Water from a Rock

We will recall that the Israelites were an onerous bunch to lead in the wilderness.[7] No sooner did God provide for their needs, then they complained about something else. On several occasions Moses has had his fill of this ingratitude and protests to God, asking God to take this burden from him.[8] On one occasion Moses even asks God to let him die, so distasteful was the task of shepherding these ingrates.[9] We will also recall that God performed a number of miracles through Moses in order to provide for the needs of the Israelites while in the desert. In fact, these miracles can be paired, one set occurring in the book of Exodus, and the other in the book of Numbers. One of these pairs of miracles is the provision of water from a rock.

In Exodus 17, God instructs Moses to take the elders with him and to stand before "the rock at Horeb." He is then told to strike the rock with his rod "and water will come out from it."[10] As expected, the strike works just as God said it would. Moses then gives the place two names, Massah, which means "testing" (since the people tested God's ability to provide for them), and Meribah, which means "contention" or "strife" (since the people contended with Moses and God about having no water).

We now fast-forward to Numbers 20. Again, the people are complaining about a lack of water, again Moses asks God what to do, and again God tells Moses to take a rod and gather the people.[11] This time, though, God does not instruct Moses to strike the rock with the rod, but simply to "speak to the rock," and water would come forth.[12] Why God would tell Moses to bring the rod if he was not supposed to use it has long baffled biblical scholars. Was this a setup? Was God making it easy for Moses to make a mistake in a moment of anger?

It seems that neither of these explanations is correct. The most compelling answer to why God would have Moses bring the rod has been proposed by William Propp, the scholar mentioned earlier in this chapter in regard to the "horns of Moses."[13] Propp traces the significance of this rod to the dispute surrounding the priesthood of Aaron found earlier in the book of Numbers. In Numbers 17 a group of Levitical priests approaches Moses and Aaron, asking why Aaron was selected as high priest and not they.[14] Aaron was no better than they, they reasoned, and they should have equal access to God. In order to demonstrate who was the legitimate high priest among the Levites, God instructed Moses to have these men give him their rods, which he was to place before the Ark of the Covenant. God intended to show them the next day who would be high priest.

The next day Moses collected the rods from before the Ark and brought them out to the people. When he showed them the rods, only Aaron's had blossomed, demonstrating that Yahweh had chosen him over his fellow Levites. God then instructed Moses and Aaron to place Aaron's rod next to the Ark so that it would be "a sign for rebels, and to end their murmurings, lest they die."[15] Thus, Propp argues, in the second narrative of bringing forth water from the rock, Moses brings that same rod before the people as a reminder of their previous rebellion. This explains why when Moses holds up the rod, this "sign for rebels," he says to the people, "Hear now, you rebels!"[16]

Moses, however, seems to have reached his limit. His words *and* actions show the very real toll that the Israelites' continual doubt and ingratitude are having on him. After gathering the people before the rock and addressing them as "rebels," Moses asks, "Shall *we* bring forth water for you from this rock?"[17] Note first that instead of speaking to the rock, Moses speaks *to the people*. God did not instruct Moses to sermonize, only to hold up the rod (which would speak for itself) and then talk *to the rock*. Note also Moses' use of the word *we*. The implication of his words is that it is not only God who will bring forth water from the rock, but, according to Moses, he himself and perhaps even Aaron are somehow responsible for what is about to happen. And, as if to further convince the people that he is an integral part of the miracle, rather than speak to the rock, he strikes it, not once, but twice! Moses has gone too far, and what follows is both unexpected and disturbing.

As the water is still flowing from the rock, presumably, and the people and their cattle are getting their fill, God speaks to Moses and Aaron in a manner quite similar to the way Moses spoke to Aaron in the wake of the deaths of Aaron's sons:

> Because you did not believe in me, *to treat me as holy in the eyes of the people of Israel,* therefore you will not bring this congregation to the land which I have given to them.
>
> NUMBERS 20:12

While the word for "to honor" *(kabad)* is not used here, its counterpart in the Nadab and Abihu story is *(qadash),* showing that the same principle is at work. Moses, who like Nadab and Abihu, was "near to [God]," did not honor God before the people. Rather he disobeyed God's specific command by striking the rock. As a result of this act of disobedience "in the eyes of the people" (recall Moses' words to Aaron, "before the people I will be honored"), God denies Moses access to the Promised Land.

Aaron, too, would suffer the same fate, for at the end of the same chapter God informs both Moses and Aaron of Aaron's impending death "because you rebelled against my command at the waters of Meribah."[18] God then commands Moses, Aaron, and Aaron's son Eleazar to ascend the steep slopes of Mount Hor where Aaron's priestly garments are to be removed and placed on his son. Once the transfer is made, Aaron dies.[19] Such is the cost of not giving honor to whom it is due, especially when it is due to God.

Honor Your Father and Mother

We now turn to the passage describing the fifth commandment, which is in a context that further defines what it means to honor one's parents.

We have already seen that "to honor" means to consider someone weighty or important. The one action that seems to demonstrate honor the most, especially in relation to God and parents, is obedience. Yet, there are some negative indicators that demonstrate one is showing a lack of honor toward someone, which this passage enumerates. Here is the full text.

> If a man has a stubborn and rebellious son, who will not listen to the voice of his father or the voice of his mother, and they discipline him, and he will not listen to them, then his father and his mother shall seize him and bring him out to the elders of his city and to the gate of his place of residence. And they shall say to the elders of his city, "This, our son, is stubborn and rebellious, he will not listen to our voice, he is a glutton and a drunkard." And all the men of his city shall stone him to death with stones. And you shall remove the evil from your midst, and all Israel shall hear and fear.
>
> DEUTERONOMY 21:18–21

While here the command violation is presented as case law, there are many obvious parallels with those violations discussed in the previous two chapters:

1. the guilty party is seized by witnesses
   (v. 19A; cf. LEV. 24:11; NUM. 15:33)
2. the guilty party is brought to a judging body
   (v. 19B; cf. LEV. 24:11; NUM. 15:33)
3. the crime is communicated to the judging body
   (v. 20; cf. LEV. 24:11; NUM. 15:33)
4. the guilty party is stoned to death
   (v. 21: cf. LEV. 24:14–16, 23; NUM. 15:35–36)

Nowhere else in Deuteronomy do we find all of these elements together. This suggests a connection between not honoring one's father and mother and our earlier stories describing the violations of the third and fourth commandments in Leviticus and Numbers, respectively. While we might hope to find an actual narrative in Deuteronomy describing the breaking of the fifth commandment, the person or persons compiling the Primary History were not given to wholesale invention; rather, they worked with the sources available to them, making only minor editorial alterations for their own literary and theological purposes. In fact, it is unlikely that such a narrative would ever exist, since it would require that parents turn their own son over to the authorities to be killed for not honoring them. This may be why the law is very careful to list specific conditions that need to be met in order to fit the criteria of not honoring one's parents. It is as though the biblical authors themselves wanted to make such a scenario an extremely rare occurrence. What kind of behavior would justify the death of one's child?

Based on the characteristics singled out by the parents when reporting their son's behavior to the elders, two seem to be at the root of his misdeeds: *stubbornness* and *rebelliousness.* A closer look at these two characteristics will give us greater insight into the problems associated with not honoring one's parents.

1. *Stubbornness:* The Hebrew word translated as "stubborn" is *sorer,* and is generally used to refer to Israel's hardness of heart toward Yahweh. In Isaiah we read of God's passionate plea to his people to quit their stubborn ways: "I stretch out my hands all day to a *stubborn* people, who walk in a way that is not good, following their own devices."[20] For the nation of Israel and, by implication, for the individual, this kind of stubbornness leads to moral corruption,[21] social injustice,[22] and eventual destruction.[23]

2. *Rebelliousness:* The Hebrew word translated here as "rebellion" is *moreh* and, like *sorer,* it is commonly used to refer to Israel's rebelliousness toward Yahweh. In fact, we have already encountered this word in the narrative of Moses' sin at Meribah. We'll remember that when Moses addresses the peo-

ple he refers to them as "rebels." And yet, because of the presumption of Moses' words ("Shall *we* bring forth water for you from this rock?") and actions (striking the rock), the tables are turned and God says of Moses, "you *rebelled* against my commands." The negative effects of rebellion on the individual, as well as on the nation, made it a particular threat to Israelite society and, therefore, required especially harsh punishment.

The result of these two characteristics in the case of this hypothetical son is *disobedience* ("he will not obey our voice") and *debauchery* ("he is a glutton and a drunkard"). We should note that the way the law reads, both the mother and the father must agree that the son is deserving of death, and both must bring the son to the elders for judgment. This seems to assure that the accusation is not simply a personal dispute between a child and one of the parents, but something both parents have experienced and believe to be a significant enough threat to the well-being of their home and/or community to require severe action. Also, before bringing the son to the elders for judgment, the parents must have made an effort to correct their son's behavior. The word used in this passage for this attempted correction, translated here as "to discipline" *(yisser),* can refer to a variety of methods of correction, from teaching to corporal punishment, and perhaps the whole spectrum of measures is intended. Yet, despite the parents' best efforts, their son continues in his stubbornness and rebelliousness and thus, the ensuing condemnation and death.

"The First Commandment with a Promise"

While the penalty for disobeying this commandment is potentially quite severe, the rewards for obeying it are quite beneficial:

Honor your father and mother, so that your days may be lengthened in the land that Yahweh your God is giving you.

EXODUS 20:12

The apostle Paul also refers to this commandment in his letter to the church at Ephesus, even making the observation that "this is the first commandment with a promise."[24] However, when Paul specifies what this promise is, there are some noteworthy differences between his account and the account in Exodus:

> Honor your father and your mother . . . so that it may be well with you *and* that you may live long on the earth.
>
> EPHESIANS 6:21

Several observations are in order here.

First, the words "that it may be well with you" are not found in the Hebrew text of Exodus 20. However, these words *are* found in the Hebrew of Deuteronomy 5:

> Honor your father and your mother as Yahweh your God has commanded you, so that your days may be lengthened and so that it may be well with you upon the land that Yahweh your God is giving to you.
>
> DEUTERONOMY 5:16

Does this mean that Paul is citing Deuteronomy? Actually, no. The issue is not which book he is citing, but which translation. Paul, as a Greek-speaking Jew writing to a Greek-speaking audience, would be more apt to cite the Septuagint (the Greek translation of the Hebrew Bible) than the Hebrew, and, in fact, the words lacking in the Hebrew of Exodus 20 *are* in the Greek of Exodus 20.

This raises an important question. Which is the original reading of Exodus 20—the shorter Hebrew text or the longer Greek text? There are at least two possibilities.

One possibility is that the Greek translators added the phrase "that it may go well with you" in Exodus 20 due to its presence in Deuteronomy 5. The translators responsible for the Septuagint are known for this kind of "filling out" of the text, and the same principle may be at work here.

However, a more likely explanation is that the longer reading "fell out" of Exodus 20 due to scribal error. Yes, biblical scribes made mistakes, and this one would have been caused by what is known as *haplography,* or literally, "writing once" that which occurs twice. In this case, the scribe's eye would have skipped from the first occurrence of "you" to the second, as the verse in the Hebrew of Deuteronomy literally reads: "that may be lengthened the days of *you* and that it may go well with *you.*" Presumably the scribe wrote the first "you" (which is only one letter in Hebrew) and then, looking back up at the original document for the "you" he had just copied, mistakenly resumed writing after the second "you," leaving out the intervening material—namely "and that it may go well with you."

Another indication that Paul is quoting from the Greek translation is that he cites these promises in the opposite order from how they appear in the Hebrew text, but in the same order as they are found in the Greek text. Looking again at the Hebrew of Deuteronomy 5, we read, "Honor your father and your mother so that [1] your days may be lengthened and [2] so that it may be well with you upon the land that Yahweh your God is giving to you." The Greek, however, reads "Honor your father and your mother [1] so that it may go well with you and [2] so that your days may be lengthened on the land the Lord your God is giving to you," which is the same order as Ephesians 6:3. Thus, with a little detective work, we are able to determine with relative certainty that Paul is quoting from the Greek and not the Hebrew text.

A Long Life: Individual or National?

It is also interesting to note where Paul chooses to end his citation of this promise. In the Hebrew Bible *and* in the Greek translation the command to honor describes the location of this long life: "on the [good] land that the Lord is giving to you." Yet, Paul ends the quotation with "on the land [or earth]," leaving out "that the Lord is giving to you." Many people reading Paul's letter might presume that the verse he quotes promises that anyone who honors his or her father and mother will live long on the earth. And perhaps this *is* how Paul understood this promise to apply in his own day, especially for a Gentile audience not living in Israel (Ephesus is located in Asia Minor, which is in modern-day Turkey). However, the original intent of this promise was not for a good and long life on earth for any particular *individual* who honors his or her mother and father, but for a good and long life *for the nation of Israel* and *in the land* God promised to Abraham, Isaac, and Jacob—the land of Canaan. That is, this is a *national* promise for Israel that they will enjoy a long existence on Israelite soil, without being harassed or exiled by foreign enemies, as long as they adhere to this commandment (and, presumably, the other nine).

The Beginning of the End

However, Israel's tenure in their land would not be as good or as long as hoped. In fact, even before Moses leaves the scene he warns the Israelites of their future disobedience to God's commandments and their inevitable dispersion among foreign nations.[25] But even this message of inescapable doom and exile is coupled with a promise of future blessing and prosperity in the land God promised to the forefathers. Moses declares:

> And it shall be that all these things will come upon you, the blessing and the curse, which I have set before you, and you will bring them to your mind in all the nations where Yahweh your God has driven you, and you will return to Yahweh your God, you and your children, and you will listen to his voice in all that I am commanding you this day, with all your heart and with all your soul. And Yahweh your God will restore your fortunes and have compassion on you, and he will gather you again from all the peoples where Yahweh your God has scattered you.
>
> DEUTERONOMY 30:1–3

But Israel's exile into foreign lands due to their covenant dis-obedience gets us ahead of our story. At present we are at the mid-point of the commandments and, not coincidentally, Deuteronomy marks the midpoint of the Primary History. Now we leave the five books of Moses and enter the Former Prophets and with them the Promised Land, where we will find our next covenant violation.

The Sixth Commandment

You shall not steal

There are only four books remaining in the Primary History, and before we reach its end, all of the remaining commandments will be broken, the walls of Samaria and Jerusalem will be breached by the Assyrian and Babylonian forces respectively, and many Israelites and Judahites will be exiled to Mesopotamia. But for now, at the midway point of our journey, things are not so grim for the Israelites. Although their great leader Moses has passed away, the Promised Land lies immediately before them, just across the Jordan River. The burden of leading the Israelites upon their conquest of Canaan now falls on the capable shoulders of Joshua. However, before we examine the fascinating history of conquest contained within the Book of Joshua, we must address an important issue: the order of commandments six through eight as listed in Exodus 20 and Deuteronomy 5.

Out of Order

Commandments six through eight are remarkably concise. Their brevity is apparent in English, as the decree "You shall not" is followed by the forbidden action, be it murder, adultery, or theft. This economy of words is more striking in the original Hebrew, with each command consisting of only two Hebrew words: the negative particle followed by the verb form. The Hebrew verbal system combines into a single word the subject pronoun and the verbal action. Thus, in commandments six through eight, the "not" of the English translation stems from the first Hebrew word *(lo')*, while the second is most accurately rendered in English as "you shall . . . (verb)." The order of these three commandments in Exodus 20 and Deuteronomy 5 is as follows:

6. You shall not murder.
7. You shall not commit adultery.
8. You shall not steal.

The first-century C.E. Jewish historian Josephus, as well as various documents from the Dead Sea Scrolls, adhere to this same order.[1]

Alternate Sequences from Egypt

Yet, the sequence above of *murder, adultery, theft* is far from universal. The Septuagint renders accurately the order of seven of the commandments as presented in the Hebrew Bible; however, commandments six through eight are listed in a different sequence. The Septuagint orders the three as follows:

6. You shall not commit adultery.
7. You shall not steal.
8. You shall not murder.

The confusion by no means stops here. Egypt played host to a discovery made in 1902 of a two-thousand-year-old document written on papyrus. The find was labeled the Nash papyrus after W. L. Nash, who purchased it from an Egyptian antiquities dealer. This remarkable find contains both the *Shema* prayer of Deuteronomy 6:4 *(Hear O Israel! The Lord our God, the Lord is one)*, as well as the Decalogue, where again the sequence of commandments six through eight differs. These three commandments according to the Nash papyrus should be ordered:

6. You shall not commit adultery.
7. You shall not murder.
8. You shall not steal.

Nash Papyrus. *The amazing discovery of the Nash papyrus in 1902 presented the oldest biblical witness prior to the Dead Sea Scrolls, as most scholars date the Nash papyrus to the late second century B.C.E. The papyrus seems to have served a liturgical purpose, as it contains two of the most important biblical passages: the Decalogue and the Shema prayer. However, the Nash papyrus maintains a different order of the Ten Commandments than that of the Hebrew Bible and Septuagint. (Illustration courtesy of Z. Radovan, Jerusalem.)*

It might be assumed that the Nash papyrus's different order resulted simply from scribal error, especially in light of the three commandments' brevity. The fact that the Nash papyrus appears to have recorded only a few important passages from Deuteronomy might lead one to conclude that the scribe may not have been as meticulously careful as those who transcribed the Hebrew Bible's actual text in its entirety. Nevertheless, scribal error does not seem to be a factor here, as two other sources written approximately one hundred years after the Nash papyrus's composition present the order of commandments six through eight in an identical fashion. Unlike the Nash papyrus, however, these two other sources are known to a much wider audience.

The first source that lists commandments six through eight as *adultery, murder, theft* comes from the Jewish philosopher Philo of Alexandria, who wrote in the first century C.E. One of his works specifically delves into the subject of the Ten Commandments, and is called appropriately enough "The Decalogue" (Greek: *deka,* "ten"; *logoi,* "words"). In this work, Philo treats the most important of ancient Israel's laws from a Hellenistic viewpoint. He uses numerology (the study of the occult meaning of numbers), gematria (the assignment of numerical values to letters and determining their significance), and other devices in an attempt to persuade the Hellenistic world of the Hebrew Bible's merit. Yet, it seems that Philo's Bible not only differs from those we read two thousand years later, but also from the Bibles used by his contemporaries—specifically, the Jewish historian Josephus and the Dead Sea Scroll community at Qumran. Like the Nash papyrus, Philo lists the prohibitions of commandments six through eight: *adultery, murder, theft.*[2]

Thus, so far we have seen three variant orders to commandments six through eight:

Exodus 20, Deuteronomy 5, Josephus, Qumran		Septuagint		Philo, Nash Papyrus	
6	Murder	6	Adultery	6	Adultery
7	Adultery	7	Theft	7	Murder
8	Theft	8	Murder	8	Theft

The Decalogue in the New Testament

The sequence adhered to by both Philo and the Nash papyrus might lead one to conclude that this variant order of *adultery, murder, theft* was peculiar to the area of Egypt. This is not the case, as the remaining witnesses to this order do not come from Egypt but Palestine.

Three separate passages in the New Testament indicate that at least three of its authors adhered to the same sequence of commands as did Philo and the author of the Nash papyrus. Jesus is reported to have said to an anonymous ruler: "You know the commandments: 'Do not commit *adultery,* Do not *murder,* Do not *steal,* Do not bear false witness, Honor your father and mother.' "[3] Consequently, the order of commandments six through eight adhered to by the author of Luke would seem to be *adultery, murder, theft.* Moreover, the placement of the command regarding parental respect last rather than fifth indicates that the order was not fixed. Interestingly, the corresponding stories in Matthew and Mark list commandments six through eight in the same order as they appear in the Hebrew Decalogue.[4] It might at first seem that Luke's variant order is random. However, the same progression of the prohibitions is found elsewhere in the New Testament, specifically in Paul's Epistle to the Romans and the Epistle of James.

The longest of Paul's letters is also his most influential. The Epistle of Paul to the Romans announces the apostle's intention of visiting the Church of Rome on his way to Spain, and allows him to explain his understanding of the gospel. The last few chapters are devoted to ethical teachings, and here we again find that commandments six through eight are ordered: *adultery, murder, theft.* Romans 13:9 reads:

> The commandments, "You shall not commit *adultery,* You shall not *murder,* You shall not *steal,* You shall not covet," and any other commandment, are summed up in the sentence, "You shall love your neighbor as yourself."

Further evidence that this order is not random comes from the Epistle of James. In chapter two James argues that to violate one commandment is to violate them all, which reflects a Jewish midrash suggesting that since the last five commandments are joined by the conjunction "and," they should be treated as one. Although only two of the three commandments under discussion are mentioned by James, they occur in the same order as Paul's list. James 2:10–11 states:

> For whoever keeps the whole law but fails in one point has become guilty of all of it. For he who said, "Do not commit *adultery*," said, "and Do not *murder.*" If you do not commit adultery but do murder, you have become a transgressor of the law.

Thus, the Nash papyrus's order of commandments six through eight is by no means an isolated case, as Philo and three passages in the New Testament confirm.

Variant Orders in the Hebrew Bible

To further the confusion, one need look no further than the Hebrew Bible itself for two other variations in the order of these three commandments. The first appears in the work of the prophet Hosea, who preached to the northern kingdom of Israel during Assyria's increasing military threat in the eighth century B.C.E. In Hosea 4:2, the prophet chastises the people for their rebellious behavior, which includes "lying, swearing, *murdering, stealing,* and *committing adultery,*" giving us a sequence without parallel.

The other variant comes from the prophet Jeremiah in his famous sermon in the Temple courtyard (Jeremiah 7). Jeremiah was a priest who prophesied in Judah both before and after the Babylonian conquest in 586 B.C.E. Prior to the Temple's destruction, Jeremiah had warned the people that just because the Temple, God's abode, stood in Jerusalem, it was not necessarily assured of God's protection. Jeremiah chastises the people's behavior as he quotes Yahweh's message to the crowd:[5]

Behold, you trust for yourselves in lying words that are use-less. Will you *steal, murder, commit adultery,* swear falsely, burn incense to Baal, and walk after other gods whom you do not know? And then come and stand before Me in this house upon which My name is called, and say, "We are saved!" only to continue doing all those detestable things? Has this house upon which My name is called become a den of robbers in your eyes? Behold, even I have seen it, declares Yahweh.

Jeremiah condemns the people for, among other command-ment violations, *theft, murder, adultery,* and bearing false witness, an order hitherto unseen.

We are left to acknowledge that these three commandments could be presented in a variety of different orders without con-fusing their connection with the Ten Commandments.

Exodus 20, Deuteronomy 5, Josephus, Qumran	Septuagint	Philo, Nash Papyrus	Hosea	Jeremiah
6 Murder	6 Adultery	6 Adultery	6 Murder	6 Theft
7 Adultery	7 Theft	7 Murder	7 Theft	7 Murder
8 Theft	8 Murder	8 Theft	8 Adultery	8 Adultery

As previously noted, these prohibitions consist merely of two words in the original Hebrew. One of the two words, the nega-tive particle *(lo'),* is the same for all three commandments. That their order would eventually differ in light of these similarities seems inevitable. There also remains the possibility that the orig-inal order of these commandments as listed in Exodus differed from that in Deuteronomy, just as we have seen other differences between these two texts, and even differences between the He-brew and Greek versions of these two texts. One may have been altered to conform to the other at a later date in an attempt to standardize their order. In fact, if we were to poll knowledgeable religious persons (even clergy), we would get a variety of orders not only for these three commandments but for the whole. The same was true for ancient Israel, even among the religiously knowledgeable.

Nonsequential Violations and Authorial Motivations

Up until now, we have seen a perfect correspondence between the order of commandment violations and books of the Primary History. For example, the second commandment was violated in the second book of the Primary History, the third in the third, and so on. Yet, the order in which commandments six through eight are violated in books six through eight of the Primary History does not match the order of Exodus 20 or Deuteronomy 5. The sixth commandment, according to Exodus and Deuteronomy, prohibits murder. The sixth book, Joshua, is filled with battles resulting in thousands of deaths, both Israelite and Canaanite, but as we shall see in the following chapter, not one of these can be classified as a murder. Furthermore, at no place in Joshua does the Hebrew word for murder used in the Decalogue occur. Likewise, the seventh commandment in Exodus and Deuteronomy forbids adultery. In Judges the closest anyone comes to committing adultery is the best man at Samson's wedding, who is given Samson's Philistine wife of one week following Samson's murder of thirty Philistine men.[6] Again, the Hebrew word for adultery used in the Ten Commandments is absent from the entire book. Finally, the eighth commandment as listed in Exodus and Deuteronomy prohibits theft. The only objects stolen in the eighth book of the Primary History are the hearts of the men of Israel by Absalom, and the bones of Saul and Jonathan from Beth-Shean by the men of Jabesh-Gilead.[7] Neither of these "thefts" warrants a loss of the land promised by God to Moses on Mount Sinai.

The reasons for the lack of conformity between the commandments as numbered in Exodus/Deuteronomy and their respective transgressions in the books of the Primary History seem simple. The chronology of many of the events described in Israel's history was set. Events during the life of Joshua preceded those of David's time, and a history indicating otherwise would be rejected out of hand. The principle of chronology is intensified by the fact that some of the events reported in the Book of Kings took place in the audience's lifetime. Thus, had the responsible party desired to compile a history in which the violations exactly matched the order of the Hebrew Decalogue, as we suppose, he would have been constrained by the fact that the sequence of many of the stories was already fixed in the narrative.

Even more important to the issue of nonconformity is the likelihood that a variant order of commandments six through eight was popular in the days of the compiler of the first nine books of the Hebrew Bible. We shall soon see that the order in which the commandments are violated in the sixth, seventh, and eighth books of the Primary History provides a clue as to the identity of the individual who created this variant order. Yet before we answer the question of *who* created the alignment of commands and violations, we must discuss the historical enterprise in ancient Israel.

The Deuteronomistic Historian and Jeremiah's Scribe

Scholars have long believed that the books of Deuteronomy, Joshua, Judges, Samuel, and Kings were compiled under the influence of a single individual. It was noticed that many of the themes, phrases, and motivations inherent to the Book of Deuteronomy continued in the Former Prophets (Joshua-Kings). Consequently, the name used by scholars to refer to this individual is the Deuteronomistic Historian, and his final product is commonly referred to as the Deuteronomistic History.

In addition, scholars have long noticed connections between the Deuteronomistic History and the Book of Jeremiah.[8] In fact, rabbinic tradition gave the authorship of Kings to this prophet, and one medieval commentator also assigned the books of Samuel to him as well. That both the Deuteronomistic History and Jere-

miah end with the same chapter (2 Kings 25 = Jeremiah 52) unequivocally demonstrates their close relationship. Remarkably
similar language and style again suggest that the Book of Jeremiah
and the Deuteronomistic History are the fruits of one person's
labors. Many scholars, including the present author, think there is
a strong possibility that the name of the Deuteronomistic Historian who compiled Deuteronomy, Joshua, Judges, Samuel, Kings,
and the Book of Jeremiah was none other than Baruch, the son
of Neriyahu, Jeremiah's scribe.[9] Baruch's vocation suited the task
of compiling his country's history. Chronology also suggests
Baruch. It would seem that the Deuteronomistic Historian wrote
the majority of his work in Jerusalem shortly before the Babylonian conquest of Judah in 586 B.C.E., which is exactly where
Baruch was situated prior to his relocation in Egypt with Jeremiah.

One of biblical archaeology's most remarkable discoveries occurred in the late 1970s, when excavations at Jerusalem unearthed
a clay seal impression bearing the inscription: "Belonging to
Baruch, son of Neriyahu, the scribe."[10]

Why the Variant Order?

We can now return to the important question of determining just
who is responsible for the fact that in the written history of Israel,
immediately after the Decalogue is received from Yahweh, the
commandments are broken one by one, book by book, until the
destruction of Jerusalem and the termination of the monarchy occur at the hands of Nebuchadnezzar, the king of Babylonia. *It is of
no small consequence that the commandments violated in the books of
Joshua, Judges, and Samuel adhere to the order in which they are listed in
the Book of Jeremiah!* This piece of evidence points to the
Deuteronomistic Historian as the person initially responsible for
the sequential pairing of command infractions and books of the
Primary History.

As we have seen, the order of the commandments was not
fixed, and different sequences were popular in different times and

The Autograph of a Biblical Author? *This clay bulla, created by the imprint of a signet ring, likely belonged to Jeremiah's scribe Baruch, the most probable candidate for the Deuteronomistic Historian. (Illustration courtesy of Bruce and Kenneth Zuckerman, West Semitic Research.)*

areas. It would seem that the order common in the days of Jeremiah listed commandments six through eight as follows: *theft, murder, adultery.* This was the order that turns up in Jeremiah's sermon in the temple courtyard.[11] The Deuteronomistic Historian was closely linked both temporally and spatially to Jeremiah, which explains why Jeremiah's sixth, seventh, and eighth commandments are violated in the sixth, seventh, and eighth books of the Primary History: Joshua, Judges, and Samuel.

So it appears that the alignment of command violations and books of the Hebrew Bible is not a mere coincidence. It was a deliberate act instigated by the Deuteronomistic Historian. By the time he sat down to compile various sources into his version of Israel's history, he was not at liberty to change the order of commandments as they appeared in Exodus 20. The sequence listed in

Commandment	Violation
You shall not steal	Joshua
You shall not murder	Judges
You shall not commit adultery	Samuel

Exodus had existed in writing as a sacred text for hundreds of years. However, when it came to editing and compiling the actual command violations in the sixth, seventh, and eighth books of the Primary History, the Deuteronomistic Historian carefully crafted the historical accounts to highlight the violations and the sequence of broken commandments as listed in Jeremiah's sermon.

Just the Deuteronomistic Historian?

It is not clear how much freedom the Deuteronomistic Historian enjoyed in creating the correlation between commands and violations. It would seem that by his time, several of the stories that relate violations of the commandments had been firmly established in the historical consciousness of the Israelites. More problematic is the fact that the Deuteronomistic Historian was apparently not responsible for composing the texts recording the first four command violations. Was it simply fortuitous that these earlier stories matched the first four commandments? Perhaps so, but it would seem that at least the third and fourth may have been inserted into the text where they are in order to fit the overall structure. The sequence of the first two violations could not have been altered by a later editor. The story of the golden calf is intimately linked to the reception of the Decalogue. Its position immediately after the ratification of the Ten Commandments creates a very dramatic effect, as Israel begins to break two of the laws immediately after receiving them. These events needed to be closely related in both time and space. However, the stories of the unnamed men who blaspheme and violate the Sabbath in Leviticus and Numbers respectively have virtually no relation to their contexts of numerous and sundry laws. They would fit equally

well anywhere in the Primary History, although most oppor-
tunely in the time of Moses.

Consequently, in addition to the Deuteronomistic Historian, it
would appear that the person responsible for the final editing of
the Primary History also had a hand in the process of aligning violations with books. This final editor combined the various
sources and ultimately decided what made it into the actual text
of the Bible as we know it. Again, it is not clear just how much
freedom the editor exercised in the Hebrew Bible's compilation.
While the final editor was certainly not at liberty to alter the general sequence of major events in his nation's history, he apparently
was capable of inserting the tales of blasphemy and the Sabbath-
breaking within the framework of laws as found in Leviticus and
Numbers. Moreover, the editor might have changed a word here
or there in various stories in order to emphasize certain violations.
Thus, as we shall see, there are several examples of murder in the
Hebrew Bible, many of which may, in fact, violate the command.
However, only one case of murder uses the exact word prohibited in the Decalogue (a very rare word), which clearly links the
violation to the command. We shall never know exactly how the
process of alignment between violations and books of the Primary
History was achieved; yet, it is quite remarkable that the end result arose through the cooperative efforts of individuals who were
separated in both time and space.

The Pattern of Commandments
and Jeremiah's Variant Order

The sequence of commandments as recorded in Exodus 20 and
Deuteronomy 5 is logical. The grouping consists of two sets of
four related ordinances, with each commandment in a set of descending magnitude.

Thus, the first four commandments concern crimes directed
against God, with the sin of apostasy being the most severe violation, idolatry next, then blasphemy, followed by Sabbath violation. The first set of four is then closed off with an order to
respect one's parents. That is, the first four commandments fall

Divine		Secular		
1. Apostasy		6. Murder		
2. Idolatry	5. Parents	7. Adultery	}	10. Coveting
3. Blasphemy		8. Stealing		
4. Sabbath		9. False Witness		

into the category of parental guidance or teaching. Commandments six through nine are secular in nature, crimes directed against society, and again the severity of each crime decreases from one command to the next. Hence the sixth commandment forbidding murder is the most serious of the four, as it concerns life. The seventh's ban on adultery protects the family, as well as the continuity of lineage. Theft, the eighth commandment, concerns the loss of property. The second set is closed off by a ban on coveting, which unlike the previous commandments, deals with motivation. As we shall see in the ninth chapter, the sin of coveting leads to the violation of commandments six through nine.

Given the pattern of descending magnitude of the commandments, what is the rationale behind the alternate order of commandments six, seven, and eight in Jeremiah, which matches the order of commandment violations in the sixth, seventh, and eighth books of the Primary History? In these books, the pattern of twin sets of four related ordinances (the first set religious, the second secular), capped by a unifying single commandment, remains consistent. However, the alternate order of *theft, murder, adultery* now requires that the theft be quite severe in order to maintain the pattern of descending magnitude in each set. As we shall see, the crime which violates theft in the Primary History's sixth book is no ordinary case of petty larceny.

The Book of Joshua:
Countless Conquests, a Single Theft

We now turn to the actual violation of the commandment prohibiting theft, found in the sixth book of the Primary History. As previously noted, this commandment consists of only two words: the negative particle followed by the second person masculine singular form of a verbal root meaning "to steal." While we might expect to encounter narratives using this word for steal, none occurs after the giving of the Ten Commandments until the sixth book of the Primary History, the Book of Joshua.

This book describes the events that transpire as the Israelites conquer the Promised Land. The story opens with the notice of Moses' death, an event that concludes the forty-year wilderness wanderings. The reins of leadership have been passed to the capable hands of Joshua, the son of Nun, whose first military campaign as leader is the mighty-walled Jericho. Two spies are dispatched across the Jordan to infiltrate Jericho, and they narrowly escape capture through the assistance of a prostitute named Rahab. In return for Rahab's aid, she is promised that her family will be saved from the annihilation that will soon follow. The spies return to the Israelite camp at Shittim, just northeast of the Dead Sea near the mouth of the Jordan River. The call is given out for the Israelites to cross the Jordan, and, in Red Sea style, the river miraculously dries up as the priests bearing the Ark of the Covenant enter, enabling the people to cross into the Promised Land. Joshua and his troops then "lay siege" to Jericho for six days. But it is not an orthodox siege, as God commands the people to march around Jericho once a day for six days, and then on the seventh to go around the city seven times. Upon completing the march, and just prior to the command to yell in unison, Joshua warns the people:

> And certainly you will avoid the devoted things, lest you be accursed by taking from the devoted things; and [you] shall make the camp of Israel become accursed and trouble it. And all the silver, and gold, and the vessels of copper and iron, they are holy to Yahweh. They shall come to Yahweh's treasury.
>
> JOSHUA 6:18–19

Which Walls Came Tumbling Down? *The site of ancient Jericho poses unique problems for finding a correspondence between the biblical text and the material record. The massive walls seen here date to the early Bronze Age, centuries before the believed time of Joshua's invasion. Later destruction levels, however, date more closely to the biblical account of Jericho's demise. (Illustration courtesy of Erich Lessing/Art Resource, N.Y.)*

Then the people shout, and at last the walls of Jericho "come tumbling down." Every living creature inhabiting the city, save Rahab and her family, is put to death. The vast majority of possessions is destroyed by fire. Presumably, only the valuable vessels of metal escape destruction, to be dedicated to Yahweh in the Israelite cultic treasury.

Joshua, believing that Yahweh's instructions have been faithfully carried out, again sends out spies, this time to the next large city: Ai. They report that only a fraction of the military force is needed to overcome the meager defenses of this city. However, disaster soon strikes the Israelites. They are thoroughly routed by the forces of Ai. Joshua falls on his face before Yahweh's ark and asks the reason for this negative turn of events. Yahweh responds,

> Israel has sinned; they have also transgressed My covenant which I commanded them, and they have also taken of the devoted things, and *stolen,* and deceived, and put it among their things.
>
> JOSHUA 7:11

Joshua is shocked to learn that one of the Israelites has been responsible for the military rout, which has brought so much suffering to their camp. The defeat at Ai has threatened the Israelite foothold in the West Bank and jeopardized the entire settlement of the land of Canaan. Now military foes will know that Israel's forces are not invincible. And, just as Yahweh says, it is all because one of His chosen people has violated His commandment against stealing.

'Urim and Thummim: Casting of Lots

The next morning, Yahweh assists Joshua in singling out the perpetrator by lot. This is accomplished, presumably, with the Israelite's most sacred tools of divination: *'urim* and *thummim.* While scholars do not know for certain, *'urim* and *thummim* appear to be two flattened stones with one side of each stone marked with the Hebrew letter *'aleph* (for *'urim,* as *'aleph* [a] is the first letter of the word *'urim),* and the other side with a *taw* (for *thummim,* as *thummim* is spelled with a *taw* [t]). Thus, they would resemble two coins, with one side of each coin bearing the symbol "heads," and the opposite side depicting "tails."

Roll the Dice. *Gaming pieces are frequently found on archaeological digs. The game board seen here, along with the die, were discovered at Tel Beit Mirsim, a site near Hebron made famous by the excavations of William F. Albright in the 1920s and 1930s. Dice were not limited to games of chance, however. They were also used to determine more dire life decisions, such as the innocence or guilt of an accused person and whether to go into battle. (Illustration courtesy of Z. Radovan, Jerusalem.)*

Sometimes *'urim* and *thummim* were dice with four or more sides, each side being illustrated with either an *'aleph* for *'urim,* or a *taw* for *thummim.*

The significance of the choice of the words *'urim* and *thummim* is twofold: first, it denotes a legal meaning. Contrary to popular opinion, *'urim* does not come from the Hebrew root *'wr,* "light."

Rather, the root is *'rr*, elsewhere used to indicate that a person is guilty or cursed. Similarly, the word *thummim* is used in a legal sense to denote innocence. The same root letters used for *thummim* are used to describe Job, which states: "There was a man in the land of Uz, whose name was Job; and this man was *innocent* and upright, and fearing God, and turning away from evil."[12] Secondly, the choice of words serves a symbolic purpose. As the word *'urim* begins with the first letter of the Hebrew alphabet, *'aleph*, and *thummim* begins with the last, *taw*, it would connote that every possibility in the universe lay between these two outcomes. A similar expression is found in Greek, where "alpha and omega" symbolizes God and/or the universe. Thus, after asking a question capable of being answered by a simple "yes" *('urim)* or "no" *(thummim)* response, the inquirer would seem to put the outcome in the hands of God. However, at least one set of pyramid-shaped dice used in ancient Egypt were fixed, as metal weights were inserted to enhance the decision!

Assuming the lots used by the Israelites were free from such devious tampering, the *'urim* and *thummim* did not always give a "yes" or "no" response. A third outcome, that of "no answer," was also a possibility. In fact, if the *'urim* and *thummim* were a pair of two-sided stones, one could expect a "no answer" response (one stone reads *'urim,* the other *thummim)* 50 percent of the time. The same would be true for dice: two dice would turn up with two *'alephs* or two *taws* 25 percent each, and one of each 50 percent of the time for a no answer.

The procedure used in selection by *'urim* and *thummim* is best exemplified by the story of Jonathan's violation of the order confirmed by Saul's oath in 1 Samuel 14. Saul orders a fast until

א א	ת ת	ת א
'Urim	*Thummim*	*Mixed*
Yes	No	No Answer

evening in an attempt to show God the devotion of the Israelites, which Saul hopes will motivate God to lend a hand in the ongoing battle against the Philistines. Upon the day's end and the fast's completion, Saul inquires of God through a priest whether or not they should attack the Philistines that very night. The priest presumably throws the 'urim and thummim, and as the stones do not match, a "no answer" is recorded. This "no answer" is taken by Saul to indicate that something has gone wrong:[13]

> And Saul said, "Draw near here all the leaders of the people, and know and see in what way this sin happened today. For as Yahweh who delivers Israel lives, surely if it is my son Jonathan, he shall certainly die." And no one answered him from all the people.

Saul has no idea that his son Jonathan, ignorant of his father's order, had earlier eaten honey, thus violating Saul's promise to Yahweh. Nevertheless, in order to reveal the perpetrator, Saul singles out himself and Jonathan from the rest of the people, asking God to give 'urim if either he or his son is guilty, and thummim if they are innocent. The answer comes as a surprise to Saul, as the reading is 'urim. Then the lots are again used to choose between Saul and Jonathan, and Jonathan is taken. Although his guilt in the matter is established, Jonathan escapes the capital punishment promised by his father when the people intervene on his behalf.

This story illustrates how the 'urim and thummim function. There is always a choice between two items. 'Urim indicates a positive response while thummim produces a negative. Finally, a "no answer" response is always an option.[14]

The Thief of Jericho

Joshua uses 'urim and thummim to discover who stole from the items collected at Jericho that were to be dedicated to Yahweh. The sacred lots end up choosing Achan, the son of Carmi. Once singled out, Achan confesses to having stolen three items: a beautiful mantle from Shinar (Babylonia), two hundred shekels of silver, and a bar of gold weighing fifty shekels.

> And Achan answered Joshua, "Of a truth I have sinned against the Lord God of Israel, and this is what I did: when I saw among the spoil a beautiful mantle from Shinar, and two hundred shekels of silver, and a bar of gold weighing fifty shekels, then I coveted them, and took them; and behold, they are hidden in the earth inside my tent, with the silver underneath."
>
> So Joshua sent messengers, and they ran to the tent; and behold, it was hidden in his tent with the silver underneath. And they took them out of the tent and brought them to Joshua and all the people of Israel; and they laid them down before the Lord. And Joshua and all Israel with him took Achan the son of Zerah, and the silver and the mantle and the bar of gold, and his sons and daughters, and his oxen and asses and sheep, and his tent, and all that he had; and they brought them up to the Valley of Achor . . . and all Israel stoned him with stones; they burned them with fire, and stoned them with stones. And they raised over him a great heap of stones that remains to this day; then the Lord turned from his burning anger. Therefore to this day the name of that place is called the Valley of Achor.
>
> JOSHUA 7:20–26

Achan and his family are put to death by stoning at the hands of the entire congregation of Israelites.

This harsh penalty of death by stoning might appear unwarranted, as elsewhere in the Israelite penal code, theft is by no means considered a capital offense. The crime of stealing is most often punished by fine and/or the imposition of damages:

> If a man steals an ox or a sheep, and kills it or sells it, he shall pay five oxen for an ox, and four sheep for a sheep. He shall

make restitution. If he has nothing, then he shall be sold for his theft.[15]

Achan's punishment is the only instance in the Hebrew Bible of an Israelite's being put to death for stealing, and it is the only case of stealing from the *herem,* what is dedicated to God.

Karet: The Apex of Penalties

Why did Achan's crime bring about the most severe of all Israelite punishments: the death of his entire family and the burning of all his belongings? In other words, complete and utter annihilation? The Hebrew word used for this punishment is *karet,* and it literally means "to cut off." When Yahweh describes himself in Exodus 34:6–7, he states that he "visits the iniquity of fathers on sons, and on sons of sons, to the third and to the fourth generation." Many see this statement as a doctrine of postponement, meaning that people can suffer for the sins of their previous relatives. However, it seems that Exodus 34 is actually referring to the punishment of all living family members. Whereas today we number parents as the first generation, the children as the second, and so on, by the Israelites' counting the children constitute the first generation, the grandchildren the second, etc. Thus, when Yahweh says that he will punish up to the fourth generation, this means that all generations alive at the time of the crime will be punished: the perpetrator, the children, the grandchildren, the great-grandchildren, and the great-great-grandchildren. This was simply their upper limit of coexisting generations, and ensured that if the crime was severe enough, the perpetrator would have no posterity. As a point of interest, this type of severe punishment is prohibited by the U.S. Constitution in Article III, Section 3, which outlaws all "bills of attainder." A bill of attainder allows capital punishment without a trial, and it was commonly used against those convicted of treason. Thus a person could be executed for being the son of a criminal. Consequently, according to the American Constitution, one cannot be held accountable for their relatives' actions. The Bible contains a similar law. Deuteronomy 24:16 declares: "Fathers shall not be put to death for children, and children shall not be put to death for fathers; each man shall be put to death for his own sin." In fact, in 2 Kings 14:6, when Joash, the twelfth king of Israel, puts to death his father's assassins but not their children, this law in Deuteronomy 24:16 is cited as the reason. The seeming contradiction between God's statement regarding punishing the third and fourth generations and the law in Deuteronomy 24 is resolved by understanding that *karet* is God's prerogative, to be used only in special cases such as Achan's.

Another example of *karet* occurs in the case of Saul and his family after he falls from Yahweh's favor. Jonathan, Saul's eldest son and heir, along with his siblings, Abinadab and Malchishua, die with their father on the field of battle.[16] Saul's son Ishbosheth succeeds to Israel's throne until he is killed in his sleep.[17] David gives Saul's two remaining sons, along with five sons belonging to Saul's eldest daughter, to the Gibeonites, who put them to death by hanging.[18] Saul's remaining daughter, Michal, who is married to David, remains childless to her death.[19] Yet, Saul's penalty is not entirely *karet,* as one of his descendants is allowed to live and procreate, Jonathan's son Mephibosheth. At times Mephibosheth comes perilously close to death, but he is repeatedly spared by David because of an earlier promise of David's to preserve Jonathan's lineage.[20]

While the process of *karet* is gradual in the case of Saul, Achan's is immediate. His genealogical line is immediately severed and he dies fully aware that his crime ended the lives of his loved ones, eliminating any chance of his perpetuating his family line. Achan's crime is the quintessential example of theft—theft from God. As a result, his sin is equivalent to the other major offenses against Yahweh as described in the first four commandments: apostasy, idolatry, blasphemy, and the breaking of the Sabbath. Consequently, the same capital punishment is merited, and in this case, the death of Achan's entire family. The events that surround all five of these transgressions against God are quite similar. Following the offense, Yahweh points out to the leaders that one of his commandments has been violated, and he then takes a direct hand in exposing the criminal and imposing the punishment.

Achan's Crime and the
Sixth Commandment: A Perfect Match

More remarkable for the task at hand is that Achan's crime is the only sin by an Israelite in the entire Book of Joshua! The only other event that even comes close is the erection of an altar by the two-and-one-half tribes (Reuben, Gad, and one half of Manasseh) residing on the eastern side of the Jordan River.[21] And as the Israelites eventually discover, the altar is an act neither of sacrilege nor of treason, as it was built only to serve as a reminder that the people should follow Yahweh. The Jordan River served as a natural boundary, and the tribes that dwelt in Transjordan believed themselves to be at a higher risk of adopting their neighbors' religions. Consequently, their action is quite the opposite of transgression, it is an attempt at preservation—the preservation of their unity with the other tribes and of their religious purity.

Thus, the only sin by an Israelite in the book of Joshua violates one of the Ten Commandments. In fact, the sin is described with exactly the same word as the commandment itself. By the reckoning of the probable compiler of this material, it is the next commandment after honoring one's father and mother. Six books, six commandments. Now on to the seventh.

The Seventh Commandment

You shall not murder

e now turn to the Book of Judges, the seventh book in the Primary History. Here we discover that the commandment prohibiting murder, the seventh commandment as enumerated in the Book of Jeremiah, is violated. And as we shall see, it is no ordinary murder.

The Book of Judges:
Conquests of Countrysides and One Heinous Homicide

The Book of Judges continues the narrative where Joshua left off. After reporting the death of Joshua, the book describes the military successes enjoyed by the tribe of Judah. Most notable in Judah's conquest is the Canaanite city of Jerusalem, where one day David will govern his empire. The text then lists the many cities and peoples that were not conquered by the tribal league but survived to dwell alongside the Israelites. This remnant of indigenous populations would soon have a negative influence on Israel. After the death of Joshua and his successors, the Israelite people are quick to forget their former allegiance to Yahweh, and begin to worship their neighbors' deities. This sets up a "quaternary cycle," as scholars refer to it, that frames the remaining narratives in the Book of Judges:

1. Israel's apostasy
2. Israel's punishment through subjugation to an enemy

3. Israel's prayer for a deliverer
4. Israel's deliverance by a judge appointed by Yahweh

This pattern is repeated several times, and serves as a background for some of the Hebrew Bible's most colorful characters: the Judges.[1]

For the ancient Israelites, the title of judge entailed responsibilities that extended beyond simply deciding legal cases. This is exemplified by an Akkadian cognate to the Hebrew word for "judge" *(shophet)*. The title of judge in the Akkadian empire was virtually synonymous with the title of king, as that person led the military, maintained harmonious relations among their subjects, and oversaw the general welfare of the nation. Similarly, the chief Punic magistrates at Carthage were titled *suffetes* (again cognate to the Hebrew *shophet)*, and they also performed multifaceted roles. However, in the Hebrew Bible, the major difference between a judge and a king would seem to be that a judge's authority is not necessarily hereditary, as is often the case in a monarchy. The one time there is an attempt to make the judgeship hereditary, in essence changing it into a kingship, the consequences are quite lethal, as we will soon see.[2]

Killing vs. Murder: Mere Semantics or Legitimate Differences?

We now turn to our next commandment, "You shall not murder," the seventh by Jeremiah's reckoning and occurring in the seventh book of the Bible. This prohibition has a far more restrictive meaning than simply forbidding the taking of another's life. The intentional killing of human beings was at times both acceptable and encouraged. If the commandment had forbidden the killing of *any* human, violations of this commandment would abound in the Book of Judges. For example, in chapter three, Eglon, the Moabite king, dies at the hands of Israel's second judge, Ehud. The next two chapters report the more famous story of a Kenite woman named Jael who drives a tent peg into the head of Sisera, the commander of the Canaanite army. In chapter seven, the Israelite men of the tribe of Ephraim kill two of the princes of Midian. Likewise, the most famous judge, Samson, kills thousands of Philistines in Chapters 14–16. However, as we shall see, none of these cases violates the commandment. They are all seen as righteous actions performed for the sake of the Israelite community and in accordance with the will of God.

It is important to recognize, therefore, that the commandment does not prohibit all forms of the taking of human life, but in fact prohibits an action that more closely corresponds to the English word *murder*. An even more accurate translation would be "You shall not commit homicide," as the Hebrew word used in the commandment (the root is *ratsach*) is elsewhere used in the legal sections of the Bible to describe both voluntary and involuntary manslaughter. This is the same word used in Deuteronomy 4:42 that describes an individual who *"murders* his neighbor unintentionally, and did not hate him in times before." In these cases, six cities of refuge were set up throughout Israel to enable such individuals to escape "blood revenge" from the surviving family members of the deceased until a trial could be held. Joshua 20:4–6 describes the procedure by which one enters and leaves these cities:

> And he shall flee to one of those cities, and shall stand at the entrance of the gate of the city, and shall declare his matter in the ears of the elders of that city. And they shall take him into the city to themselves, and shall give him a place, and he shall live with them. And if the avenger of blood pursues him, then they shall not deliver the manslayer into his hand, for he has struck his neighbor without knowing, and did not hate him yesterday and the day before. And he shall live in that city until he stands before the congregation for judgment, until the death of the high priest who is in those days. Then the manslayer shall return and come to his city, and to his house, to the city from where he fled.

So, while the word used in the Decalogue can cover the entire range between involuntary manslaughter and murder in the first degree, the presence of these six cities of refuge seems to indicate that the commandment only applies to first-degree murder, that is to say, murder with malice or forethought.

From other passages it becomes clear that this command applies almost exclusively to personal relations between Israelites, as the killing of Israel's enemies in war is almost always a commendable action, including, at times, women and children, though this is much rarer. In these cases, to spare even one of the enemy could bring a curse on the entire Israelite community. Such is the case in 1 Samuel 15:3, when Samuel relays Yahweh's message to Saul concerning Israel's bitter enemy, the Amalekites:

> Now go, and you shall strike Amalek and destroy all that he has. And you shall have no pity on him, and you shall put to death all from man to woman, from child to infant, from ox to sheep, from camel to ass.

In fact, when Samuel discovers that Saul has spared one of the Amalekites, King Agag, he denounces Saul and dispatches the king himself.

Another type of killing that does not fall under the category of murder is capital punishment. Several crimes, according to the Hebrew Bible, warrant a penalty of death. Most of these are crimes against Yahweh and the realm of the sacred. Others expressly violate one of the commandments. Such is the crime of murder. Exodus 21:14 states, "If a man seethes against his neighbor, to kill him by deceit, you shall take him from my altar [in the city of refuge] to die." Most often the executor of capital punishment would be those seeking blood revenge: the victim's family. Yet, the individual who carries out the death penalty does not violate the commandment prohibiting homicide.

Thus, a violation of the commandment prohibiting murder would need to meet the following criteria: the victim must not be an Israelite enemy, the death cannot be the result of suicide (assisted or self-inflicted), or capital punishment, and the murder must not result from self-defense, the defense of others, or an accident. There are three events recorded in the Book of Judges that satisfy these categories, but only one, as we shall see, is a perfect fit.

Fratricide and Filicide

One action that does seem to constitute murder occurs early in Judges 9, and it reflects Israel's difficult transition from a tribal league to a monarchy. Gideon, a judge from the tribe of Manasseh, is able to break the Midianite suppression of Israel. The people then offer Gideon the position of king, which Gideon rejects.[3] Following Gideon's death, his son Abimelek proves to be more ambitious than his father. Abimelek kills all but one of his seventy brothers in order to secure the position of king formerly offered to his father. Judges 9:5 states: "And he [Abimelek] went into his father's house at Ophrah, and *killed* his brothers, the sons of Jerubbaal, seventy men on one stone." The verb used here has a more general sense of "killing" (from the Hebrew root *harag),* and it is used not only for murder but for all types of killings, including the killing of animals. Thus, at no time is the Hebrew word for *murder* that is used in the Decalogue found in this story. Moreover, the elimination of rival claimants to Israel's most sovereign office is not clearly defined as a criminal action.

History clearly indicates that one of the key problems with governments in which the supreme power is hereditary is that the positions are far from secure while rival heirs remain alive. Knowing this, Richard III in Shakespeare's drama imprisoned and killed his nephews in order to ensure his royal authority in England. The historical reality is of course much more complicated. While the princes were held in the Tower, Parliament declared both of them to be the illegitimate sons of Edward IV, Richard III's older brother and predecessor. That left Richard as the only legitimate claimant to the throne. So strictly speaking he had no need or cause to put the princes to death, although if they had lived, supporters of Edward IV might well have tried to establish their claim. In fact, the older son, Edward, was called Edward V even though he never reigned. The next Edward to occupy England's throne, the son of Henry VIII, was called Edward VI. So while the picture regarding Richard's actions in the matter remains cloudy, the fact remains that Richard's expected regnal tenure increased dramatically upon the deaths of the potential heirs.[4] The same holds true for the Hebrew Bible. One book after Abimelech's purge, both David and Solomon eliminate rivals to the throne, and both actions apparently go unpunished. And again, the Hebrew word for murder used in the Decalogue is absent from both narratives.

Another possible case of murder is found in Judges 11. Here, Jephthah vows to sacrifice to Yahweh the first thing that passes through his door upon his return home if only God will give him success in his military campaign against the Ammonites. Archaeology informs us that animals were frequently tied to the doorposts of Israelite houses, and so Jephthah's promise is perhaps not so foolish as it initially seems. Unfortunately for Jephthah, his daughter, an only child, is the first to exit his house in order to meet him.[5] Had Jephthah not performed this grievous sacrifice and broken his vow, he would have violated the third commandment of lifting up Yahweh's name in vain, as he had made an oath to Yahweh. So it is not so clear whether the commandment prohibiting murder was violated, especially since once again the Hebrew word for murder used in the Decalogue is absent from this story. In fact, the Hebrew word for murder is used rather sparingly. Even in the Primary History's most famous case of murder, where Abel dies at the hands of his brother Cain, the more common word for killing is used once again, while the word for murder is absent. So while there are indeed a few cases of murder that fit the Israelite definition, the absence of the same word used in the Ten Commandments narrows our focus to only one story.

The Murder of a Concubine

It seems to be more than a coincidence that the first time any form of the Hebrew word meaning "to murder" is used in narrative after the giving of the Ten Commandments is in the Book of Judges. Judges 19–21 tells the story of a Levite who quarrels with his concubine, after which she returns to her father's house in Bethlehem. Four months later, the Levite leaves his home in the hills of Ephraim and travels to Bethlehem to be reconciled with the woman. It turns out that he gets along famously with her father, and every time the Levite sets out to return home with his concubine, he is coaxed by her father into staying another night in Bethlehem. On the evening of the fifth day of his stay at the father's house, the Levite and concubine set out for home as the sun begins to go down. They make it as far as Gibeah, a city near Jerusalem belonging to the tribe of Benjamin, where they have trouble finding a room.

Eventually an elderly man graciously invites them to spend the night at his home. However, not all the inhabitants of Gibeah are so cordial. Soon a mob of unruly men surrounds the house and beats on the door, demanding to see the stranger who has just come to their town. They shout to the elderly man, who refuses to open the door, "bring out the man who came to your house, and we will know him."[6] While it may seem harmless enough just to want to get to "know" this wayfarer, the implication of their words is that they want to know him in a sexual sense, as what follows makes clear. The master of the house vainly attempts to placate the crowd, retorting: "No, my brothers, please do not be so evil! After all, this man came to my house, do not do this vile thing!"[7] The magnitude of the situation is graphically displayed in the following lines, where the master of the house feels the need to resort to drastic action. Rather than turn over his Levite guest to the rabid people, he offers the concubine and even his own daughter to the mob, stating, "Behold, my virgin daughter and his concubine, I will bring them out now. Ravish them and do to them what is good in your eyes, but to this man, do not do this vile thing!"[8] The crowd persists, and so the Levite quickly seizes his concubine and places her outside.[9] The crowd subsequently ravishes the girl throughout the night. The violence proves excessive, and the next morning the Levite finds her dead on the doorstep.

This was no ordinary crime, which perhaps explains the extraordinary events that follow. The Levite puts her corpse on his donkey and carries her home to the hills of Ephraim. Once there, he dismembers her corpse into twelve pieces and sends one to each of the twelve tribes of Israel. Needless to say, this action gets the attention of the nation, and the leaders of the tribes assemble to hear the details of this crime committed by the inhabitants of Gibeah. The action is described as the worst in Israel's history. Judges 19:30 states, "There has not happened, nor has there been seen anything like this since the day that the Israelites went up from the land of Egypt until this day."

The tribe of Benjamin, to which Gibeah belongs, refuses to help the confederation apprehend and punish the perpetrators, which brings the tribal league very near to destruction. Civil war ensues, resulting in many casualties:

> And there came against Gibeah ten thousand picked men out of all Israel, and the battle was hard; but the Benjaminites did not know that disaster was close upon them. And the Lord defeated Benjamin before Israel; and the men of Israel destroyed twenty-five thousand one hundred men of Benjamin that day; all these were men who drew the sword. So the Benjaminites saw that they were defeated . . . But when the signal began to rise out of the city in a column of smoke, the Benjaminites looked behind them; and behold, the whole of the city went up in smoke to heaven. Then the men of Israel turned, and the men of Benjamin were dismayed, for they saw that disaster was close upon them. Therefore they turned their backs before the men of Israel in the direction of the wilderness; but the battle overtook them and those who came out of the cities destroyed them in the midst of them. Cutting down the Benjaminites, they pursued them and trod them down from Nohah as far as opposite Gibeah on the east. Eighteen thousand men of Benjamin fell, all of them men of valor . . . So all who fell that day of Benjamin were twenty-five thousand men that

drew the sword, all of them men of valor . . . And the men of Israel turned back against the Benjaminites, and smote them with the edge of the sword, men and beasts and all that they found. And all the towns which they found they set on fire.

JUDGES 20:34–48

The feud is finally resolved, though the toll is heavy. The account concludes, "And the people had compassion on Benjamin because the Lord had made a breach in the tribes of Israel" (Judges 21:15). This is the final story in the Book of Judges, as though to illustrate that the seriousness of the crime of murder serves as the culmination of the narrative of Judges. And while *karet* is not in fact implemented, the punishment is not far removed from it.

While numerous crimes may be derived from this narrative, only one of the Ten Commandments is specifically violated—murder. Not only does the murder of the Levite's concubine fit the strictures of this commandment, but the same Hebrew word for murder *(ratsach)* used in the commandment is found here. Judges 20:4 refers to the concubine as "the *murdered* woman."

The story of the murdered concubine is illustrative of a crucial point regarding the role of the Israelite community as well as the individual. The Ten Commandments are clearly aimed at individuals; they are all worded so that the subject is the second person singular "you." However, the community is required to see that the commands are enforced and that violations are punished. If for any reason the individual is not held accountable for his or her crime, the entire community becomes guilty. This is what happened in the Book of Joshua, when Achan's unpunished crime caused the Israelite army's defeat at Ai. It was not until Achan faced his charges that the community, relieved of further responsibility, was spared further punishment. This is also why the entire Israelite community must seek out and execute Sabbath violators, blasphemers, and seriously disobedient and rebellious children. Benjamin, as the tribe where the crime took place, should have exercised responsibility by arresting and punishing the violators.

By failing to do so, they became accomplices with the criminals and equally guilty with them. Consequently, the entire Israelite tribal confederacy goes to war against the tribe of Benjamin, as they must punish the concubine's murderer or face divine punishment themselves.[10]

Once again, based on Jeremiah's order of commandments six through eight, we find the seventh commandment violated in the seventh book of the Primary History. The murder of the Levite's concubine in Gibeah is a paradigmatic violation of the corresponding command. Only two books remain in the Hebrew Bible's Primary History, as ancient Israel gradually approaches foreign conquest and subsequent exile.

The Eighth Commandment

You shall not commit adultery

Our journey now leads us to the eighth book of the Primary History: the Book of Samuel. In the initial book, Genesis, God promised Abraham that "kings shall come from you."[1] In the Book of Samuel, many generations later, we find the fulfillment of that promise when Saul is anointed the first king of Israel. Israel's transformation from a tribal confederacy into a monarchy largely results from the need to maintain military strength under a permanent centralized command in order to meet the military prowess of the Philistines. After all, the Philistines repeatedly defeat the Israelite forces and at one point even capture Israel's most sacred possession: the Ark of the Covenant.[2] While the Ark is eventually returned to Israel, the people think a more centralized form of government is needed to end this string of defeats on the battlefield. Even though they are warned that kings will conscript their sons into the military, procure their daughters to be palace servants, and take one tenth of their crops and livestock, the people remain steadfast in their demand for a king. Samuel, the final Israelite judge, is not happy with the request. Neither is Yahweh. When Samuel prays concerning the people's wishes, Yahweh responds in 1 Samuel 8:7, "Listen to the voice of the people in all that they say to you; for they have not rejected you, but they have rejected me from being king over them." But just how does the formation of a monarchy reject Yahweh's leadership?

The Israelite Monarchy
and the Separation of Church and State

Upon their initial conquest and settlement of their promised land, Israel had been governed by a tribal league led by a long series of judges, an office that as we learned in the last chapter goes well beyond the confines of deciding cases. Judges in the Hebrew Bible at times act as priests, prophets, political administrators, and military leaders. Samuel, for example, performs the priestly functions at the main sanctuary in Shiloh, acts as a prophet mediating between Yahweh and the people, and politically governs the tribal league. The people now demand in effect a separation of church and state, where the office of king will control the political and military spheres, while the priests and prophets will see to the community's religious needs. Nevertheless, the secular and religious offices remain in close contact, creating a system of checks and balances. Israelite monarchs will always be dependent upon priests and prophets, as exemplified by Saul's eventual fall from power when he loses favor with Samuel.

Saul's procurement of the throne is dependent upon Samuel's willingness to anoint him in the first place. Following the anointing, Saul's reign goes rather well for about a week, that is, until Saul makes two terrible mistakes, both of which involve disobeying Samuel's instructions. Immediately after anointing Saul king, Samuel gives him specific directions to await his arrival at the cult center of Gilgal for seven days, when Samuel promises to arrive and make sacrifices to Yahweh, after which they can engage the Philistines in battle. Saul arrives at Gilgal, but he and his forces grow impatient amidst the ever-increasing military presence of the Philistines. On the seventh day, Saul decides to take matters into his own hands, and performs the sacrifices himself.[3] Saul's ill-advised move meets with serious repercussions. Just as the sacrifices near completion, Samuel arrives at Gilgal and is furious at Saul's encroachment upon his prerogatives as priest and prophet. He informs Saul in 1 Samuel 13:13–14 that while Saul and his descendants could have ruled Israel forever, now Yahweh has chosen someone else to be king. Unfortunately, Saul, it seems, is not one to learn from his mistakes, as just two chapters later he again violates one of Samuel's orders. Samuel conveys to Saul Yahweh's wish to destroy all the Amalekite people and livestock,[4] but Saul spares the Amalekite king Agag and the choicest animals. Samuel wastes no time in denouncing Saul and pronouncing irrevocable judgment upon him. Then Samuel marches off to Bethlehem, where under Yahweh's direction he anoints the young shepherd boy David to replace Saul as king. This story illustrates that Yahweh's role in the political sphere remains powerful indeed through the work of priests and prophets, despite the advent of the Israelite monarchy.

King David: Kingship by Divine Right

Saul eventually dies in battle against the Philistines, and following a civil war between David and one of Saul's surviving children, David emerges victorious. Over time, David becomes arguably the best king ever to sit on Israel's throne. His military ability is unsurpassed by later Israelite leaders, and his kingdom reaches the furthest boundaries of Israel's monarchical period. He is also a very gifted diplomat. For example, when the time comes to set up a capital over his united kingdom, he chooses not his native home of Bethlehem, but a newly conquered city outside the tribal boundaries: Jerusalem. Thus the new capital city's location will not favor one tribe over another. Furthermore, not only was David talented in the realms of military science and diplomacy, he also benefited from a brilliance unparalleled by any other biblical king. While 1 Kings 4:29–31 states that David's son Solomon was the wisest person ever to live, David's intellect in many respects overshadows his son's. David also possessed an invaluable asset when it came to politics: he was divinely favored. Even though slings are formidable weapons, and Goliath did make a big target (1 Samuel 17:4 reports that Goliath's height was six cubits and a span tall, or nine feet nine inches!—although the Septuagint records a more reasonable height of six feet nine inches), David's good fortune enabled him to fell the giant with his first stone. The strike was indeed propitious, as David was not wearing armor and Goliath's spear weighed over six hundred shekels of iron, or nearly twenty pounds (1 Samuel 17:7). And as if all these qualities were not enough, David's poetical and musical talents were unrivaled, and 1 Samuel 16:12 further informs us that he had red hair, beautiful eyes, and was handsome. The women loved him. The men loved him. Then one spring evening while walking on his roof David happened to spy a woman bathing, and he proceeded to get into some *really* serious trouble. But before we examine the lurid details of how this most famous of biblical kings violates the eighth commandment, some words on the order of books in the Hebrew Bible are necessary. As in many Bibles, the eighth book is not Samuel, but Ruth.

Later Orders and Divisions of Biblical Books

In the Septuagint and in most English translations of the Bible, the Book of Ruth immediately follows Judges, making Samuel the ninth book. However, this is a secondary development, based on chronological events that the Book of Ruth purports to record. In the Book of Ruth, Ruth gives birth to Obed, whose fame arises solely from his grandson: King David. The original Hebrew canon places Ruth within the Five Rolls (in Hebrew, *megillot)*, along with Song of Songs, Ecclesiastes, Lamentations, and Esther. Subsequent producers of the biblical canon thought that stories concerning David's great-grandmother would be better situated just prior to David's own exploits in the Book of Samuel. Also, the Book of Ruth begins with the words "In the days when the Judges judged . . . ," which was a clue to put the book next to the Book of Judges.

Josephus explains the attachment of both Ruth to Judges and Lamentations to Jeremiah as a result of number crunching to achieve numerical symbolism. There are twenty-four letters in the Greek alphabet, and it is no coincidence that the most esteemed books in the Hellenistic world, the *Iliad* and the *Odyssey,* each contain twenty-four books. In fact, there are also twenty-four books in the Hebrew Bible. However, Josephus has a vested interest in getting the number down to twenty-two, which is the number of letters in the Hebrew alphabet. Thus he states that the Jewish faith possesses:

> Twenty-two books which contain the records of all the past times, which are correctly believed to be divine. And of them five belong to Moses . . . From the death of Moses to the reign of Artaxerxes king of Persia . . . [the prophets] wrote what occurred in their lifetimes in thirteen books. The remaining four books contain hymns to God, and precepts for the conduct of human life.
>
> AGAINST APION, I.39

Josephus' statement is a bit enigmatic, but it seems to break down as follows:

Moses' five books: Genesis, Exodus, Leviticus, Numbers, Deuteronomy.

Prophets' thirteen books: Joshua, Judges, Samuel, Kings, Isaiah, Jeremiah, Ezekiel, Book of the Twelve, Chronicles, Ezra-Nehemiah (one book), Daniel, Esther, and Job.

Four hymns to God: Psalms, Proverbs, Song of Songs, Ecclesiastes.[5]

This leaves two books unaccounted for, Ruth and Lamentations. For Josephus' model to work, he must attach Ruth to Judges and Lamentations to Jeremiah. So Ruth and Lamentations are not counted separately but as parts of the preceding books. Only then is the number reduced from twenty-four to twenty-two. Nevertheless, the fact remains that in the original Hebrew Bible, there are twenty-four books, and more important for our purposes, Judges immediately precedes Samuel. They are consequently the seventh and eighth books respectively of the Primary History.

Other variations resulted from later translations of the Bible. Samuel in the original Hebrew is not divided into two sections; it remains one book: in the original, there is no such thing as 1 Samuel and 2 Samuel; there is only Samuel. The same is true for the Book of Kings and the Book of Chronicles. All three were divided at a later date, presumably upon the Septuagint's creation. The Greek translation of the Bible is considerably longer than the original. Greek uses a full set of vowels, whereas Hebrew only used occasional vowel letters to represent long vowels. Also, Hebrew does not separate single letter words like the conjunction "and" *(waw)* or the definite article "the" *(heh)* from the preceding word, as do Greek and other languages. Moreover, two or more Greek words are often required to accurately render a single word in Hebrew. While the invention of the book permitted lengthy works to be bound to one another, at the time of the Septuagint's completion in the second century B.C.E., the innovation of the book had not yet seen the light of day. The newly expanded length of the Greek translations of Samuel, Kings, and Chronicles exceeded the spatial limits allowed by scrolls. It is no coincidence that Samuel, Kings, and Chronicles are the longest books of the Bible, each containing approximately 25,000 Hebrew words. The Greek runs to 37,000–38,000, or about 50 percent longer than the original Hebrew. Therefore, the Greeks simply divided their translation into two sections, with 1 Samuel on one scroll and 2 Samuel on the other.[6]

Adultery in the Bible

The eighth commandment by our count prohibits adultery. The modern definition of adultery generally takes into consideration the marital status of both the male and female participants, as state laws vary. This is not the case in the Hebrew Bible. Adultery in the Bible consists of sexual relations between a married woman and any man other than her husband. The marital status of the man is of no concern. Also, biblical adultery requires sexual intercourse. Without that, whatever the consenting couple does is not adultery, though it may still be punishable. While passages such as Malachi 2:10–16 and Proverbs 5:15–20 criticize male infidelity, such behavior is penalized to a much lesser extent. Biblical adultery is a capital offense requiring the death penalty for both participants.[7]

Ancient Israel was a potentially polygamous society in that legally, nothing except finances prohibited a man from taking more than one wife. As an extreme example, Solomon in 1 Kings 11:3 is reported to have seven hundred wives and three hundred concubines. Nevertheless, these royal marriages were conducted for diplomatic purposes, and for the patriarchs and the average Israelite, one or, more rarely, two wives would seem to be the norm. For example, Samuel's father, Elkanah, had two wives, because the first one, Hannah, the one whom he loved, was barren. Therefore, he took Peninnah to be his second wife.[8]

Penalties for Adultery, Premarital Sex, and Rape

The penalty for adultery is harsh in the Bible. Both participants are put to death. Leviticus 20:10 states, "If a man commits adultery with the wife of his neighbor, both the adulterer and the adulteress shall surely be put to death." A similar law can be found in Deuteronomy 22:22. The sexual promiscuity of a betrothed woman with any man other than her intended is treated in a similar manner, with capital punishment employed for violation. Nevertheless, Deuteronomy 22:23–27 distinguishes between the rape of a betrothed woman and intentional infidelities. The law states that if a betrothed woman has sexual relations with another man in a city, and does not cry out for help, then both participants are to be put to death. But if the sexual relations take place outside of the city, then only the man is to be put to death, because no one was around to hear the woman cry out for help. Thus, if the betrothed woman makes an attempt to resist, it is considered rape, and only the man suffers capital punishment.

Lesser penalties apply in the Bible for a couple who engages in sex willingly before the young woman's betrothal. Exodus 22:16–17 reads:

> If a man seduces a virgin who is not betrothed, and lies with her, he shall surely pay her dowry for a wife to himself. If her father utterly refuses to give her to him, he shall pay silver equivalent of the dowry of virgins.

Clearly, a woman's status in the biblical world at times left a great deal to be desired. The sexual experience of a daughter drastically lowered her value. No mention is made of the girl's torment following her seduction; the law only requires the perpetrator to make financial compensation to her father. One reason for the emphasis placed upon virgin brides, along with the harsh punishments toward unfaithful wives, is a grievous fear of mistaken paternity. In the patrilineal world of the Bible, identity was intimately linked to the father, and it was to the father that an individual owed his or her livelihood, honor, and inheritance. It was imperative to the society of the biblical world that there be no doubt as to who begot a child. Nevertheless, to judge the Bible's conception and treatment of women by modern standards is not entirely fair. When placed in the context of the ancient Near East, many of the laws concerning women were quite enlightened. Israelite women could divorce, inherit property, and in cases such as Deborah or Athaliah, run the entire country.

Adulterous Israelites

Let us now return to the Primary History and examine the possible contenders for the violation of the above commandment. There are five incidents in Genesis where characters are thought by others to be guilty of adultery. But as we shall see, not one of these cases explicitly violates the command. Both Abraham and Isaac attempt to pass their wives off as sisters in order to spare themselves physical harm. Genesis 12:10–20 describes a great famine in the land of Israel, which forces Abraham to look elsewhere for food. He journeys south to Egypt, where he tells Sarah,

> Behold please, I know that you are a beautiful woman to look upon. And it will be, when the Egyptians see you, then they will say: "This is his wife;" and they will kill me, and they will save you alive. Please say that you are my sister, so that it may be well with me because of you, and my soul shall live because of you.

At least part of Abraham's prediction turns out to be accurate: Sarah's beauty is well received in Egypt. Ultimately, she is taken into Pharaoh's harem, and Abraham is given many valuable items including slaves, cattle, donkeys, and camels, in return for his "sister's" favors. All does not end well for Pharaoh. Yahweh sends a great plague on the entire royal house of Egypt, and Pharaoh at last discovers Abraham's ploy. Abraham and his wife are sent away, but without reprisal, and they presumably leave with the gifts Pharaoh had previously bestowed on Abraham.

Whether or not Sarah engaged in sexual intercourse with Pharaoh is not made explicit by the text. In any case, a similar tale in Genesis 20 makes a point of stating that Sarah's relationship with a foreign king was not consummated. Here Abraham again claims Sarah is his sister to avoid bodily harm, although this time the fabrication occurs in Gerar, a city near Gaza that will eventually be part of the Philistines' territory. The king's name is Abimelek. After Sarah is taken into his house, Abimelek has a dream in which Yahweh visits him and warns him of imminent death unless Abraham's wife is returned. Genesis 20:4 specifies that "Abimelek had not come near her."

A scenario similar to the above two takes place in Genesis 26:1–11, a passage we briefly explored in chapter one. The foreign king is again Abimelek, although this time he is not warned by Yahweh of Isaac's deception. The king happens to witness for himself Isaac fondling Rebekah, from which he rightly concludes that Isaac and Rebekah are not siblings. Abimelek is upset to have so narrowly escaped tragedy resulting from a traveler's deception. He sends Isaac away, but again the patriarch goes largely unpunished. Just as in the previous account, it is made explicitly clear that no man save Isaac ever touched Rebekah (Genesis 26:10).

The fourth case of suspected marital infidelities in Genesis occurs in chapter 38. Judah has three sons, Er, Onan, and Shelah. The firstborn Er takes a wife named Tamar, but the text states that "Er was wicked in the sight of Yahweh; and Yahweh slew him" (Genesis 38:7). Onan was then required to marry his brother's childless widow to continue Er's line as dictated by levirate marriage customs (Deuteronomy 25:5–10). However, while Onan is having relations with Tamar, he withdraws and spills "his seed on the ground" (Genesis 38:9). This again displeases Yahweh, who slays Onan as well. By this time Judah is getting nervous, as he has only one son left. Judah stalls for time by telling Tamar to return to her father's house to give Judah's youngest son Shelah time to grow up. Time passes, and Tamar has grown impatient waiting for Judah to fulfill his obligation of providing her with another husband. When she learns that Judah will be in the area of her father's house, she decides to trick him. But this is no ordinary ruse. She dresses up as a prostitute and is disguised so that her father-in-law will not recognize her. Tamar, playing the role of the prostitute, asks Judah what he will give in payment. Judah promises a kid from the flock, but his word is not good enough for Tamar. She demands as collateral Judah's staff, and more important, his seal and cord (38:18). Such seals were the checks of the ancient Near East, as they allowed people to avoid paying on the spot by pledging to pay later. Each cylinder seal was unique, and when rolled upon a soft material such as clay, the surface was marked with the bearer's symbol. Thus, the process was similar to modern signatures on checks. After securing Judah's seal, Tamar agrees to have sex with him.

Lo and behold, Tamar conceives (twins!) and three months later, she is showing. Judah learns of this and is furious, as Tamar was required to abstain from sex while she waited for Judah's youngest son. Judah orders Tamar to be burned on the charges of "harlotry." This is a very serious accusation, carrying the death penalty. Deuteronomy 22:23–24 treats a betrothed woman similarly to a married woman, in that capital punishment is called for when either has sexual relations with a man other than her fiancé or husband. However, while the punishments are the same, Tamar did not commit adultery. Tamar tells her father-in-law in 38:25 that "By the man to whom these belong I am with child," showing Judah his seal and cord, along with his staff. Judah realizes that he was in the wrong for withholding his son, and remarkably exclaims, "She is more righteous than I" (Genesis 38:26). Thus, it seems that Tamar goes unpunished. In fact, Judah takes her into his house. While she should have been betrothed to Shelah, Tamar's status remains that of a widow for the rest of her life, and she has no further sexual relations with Judah. Moreover, at the time of their sexual encounter, Tamar is not married, but betrothed. Consequently, once again the crime of adultery as conceived in the Bible did not occur.

The fifth case of suspected infidelity in Genesis occurs in the following chapter, when Joseph is wrongfully accused of adultery by Potiphar's wife. Joseph has been left for dead by his brothers, is picked up by some desert travelers, and is sold to an Egyptian official named Potiphar. Joseph does very well in Egypt, and after a time he virtually runs all of Potiphar's affairs. Potiphar's wife longs to be intimate with Joseph, but the latter refuses her advances. She at last sets him up, and frames him for attempted rape. The text is clear that in light of the woman's false accusations, no intercourse occurred. Yet again the commandment is not violated, as adultery did not take place.

Thus in Genesis, the only possible case of a violation against the commandment forbidding adultery takes place when Abraham gives Sarah to Pharaoh, and this is not clear. Ignorance may be an excuse since Pharaoh was not told that Sarah was married. More important, these stories take place prior to the giving of the law on Mount Sinai, so one can hardly violate a commandment before one knows what it is.

In addition to the aforementioned cases in Genesis, references to adultery abound in the Latter Prophets (Isaiah-Malachi). Here, Israel's relation to Yahweh is often compared to that of an adulterous woman. The prophets claim that God has been a righteous husband, and Israel has sought after other gods. Jeremiah 5:7 claims,

> How can I pardon you? Your children have forsaken me, and have sworn by those who are no gods. When I fed them to the full, they committed adultery and trooped to the houses of harlots.

The sin of adultery is here an analogy, not a clear infraction.

There is only one case of adultery in the Hebrew Bible where the crime, the participants, and the events surrounding it are all made explicit. It is also one of the most famous cases of adultery in all literature.

David and Bathsheba

When we left David early in this chapter to explore the Hebrew Bible's meaning of adultery and the other possible contenders for this command violation, things were going pretty well for Israel's most gifted king; but all that changed when he saw Bathsheba bathing. Bathsheba was not engaged in an ordinary bath when David spied her out. She was undertaking a ritual bath to cleanse herself following her menstrual period (2 Samuel 11:4). This makes it explicitly clear that she is not pregnant when David sends for her. The text is also explicit in that David proceeds knowing full well that Bathsheba is married to Uriah the Hittite; he knows he is committing adultery. David's sin is further exacerbated when it turns out that Uriah, while called a "Hittite," is a loyal follower of Yahweh and David, his commander-in-chief. In fact, at the time when David has intercourse with Bathsheba, Uriah is off

"The House of David." *This inscription, found at Tel Dan in northern Israel, and dating to mid-ninth century* B.C.E., *provides the earliest evidence for the existence of King David. The author of this inscription seems to boast of killing the kings of Israel and Judah, which he calls "The House of David," a common way of referring to a dynasty in the ancient Near East. (Illustration courtesy of Z. Radovan, Jerusalem.)*

fighting the Ammonites on David's behalf. This Hittite man is more virtuous than David, God's own anointed. Thus again and again the story's details focus on the gravity of David's command violation. But as is well known, David commits adultery, sends Bathsheba home, and eventually hears the news: she has conceived a child.

David's Plan of Absolution

David is not one to give up so quickly in the face of adversity. He comes up with a seemingly foolproof plan to resolve the situation. He sends for Uriah, who promptly returns home from the battle, and David instructs him to go home for the night, trusting that Uriah's passions will result in an encounter which will reduce

Uriah's surprise when he would later hear of his wife's pregnancy. Yet, despite David's ingenuity, no one could have anticipated Uriah's incredible level of piety. Uriah does not go home that night; rather, he sleeps at the door of David's palace. When asked by David why he did not go home, Uriah responds:

> The ark and Israel and Judah dwell in booths; and my lord Joab and the servants of my lord are camping in the open field; shall I then go to my house, to eat and to drink, and to lie with my wife? As you live, and as your soul lives, I will not do this thing.
>
> 2 SAMUEL 11:11

Uriah's avoidance of sexual relations is in accordance with the rules of Holy War, as warriors consecrated for battle must abstain from sex. David himself knows this law. He earlier tells the priests of Nob that his soldiers may have no contact with women while on expeditions (1 Samuel 21:5).

David tries his plan one more night, this time spending a great deal of effort in getting Uriah intoxicated, and then sending him home, trusting that the powers of wine will let down Uriah's guard. David's efforts again are to no avail: Uriah remains impeccable, Bathsheba sleeps alone, and David is still on the hook.

Then David dramatically multiplies the severity of his sin by devising a plan to cover his tracks. He will get rid of Uriah. David composes an order for his military commander Joab to put Uriah in the front of the battle line, and then to suddenly withdraw the other troops, leaving Uriah exposed. Ironically, it is Uriah who carries his own death warrant to David's general. Joab reads the letter and complies with David's wishes. This time David's plan succeeds, and Uriah is killed in battle. Bathsheba is then free to marry David, and she bears him a son. This is the most famous case of adultery in literature, and certainly the clearest and most heinous case of adultery in the Bible; it unequivocally violates our eighth commandment.

A Punishment Fit for a King

While David as king is the most powerful person in Israel, the system of checks and balances between the religious and secular spheres of government results in David's actions meeting with severe penalties. This time the prophet Nathan makes known Yahweh's disappointment to David in his famous parable of the poor man's lamb. 2 Samuel 12:1–5 states,

> "There were two men in a certain city, the one rich and the other poor. The rich man had very many flocks and herds; but the poor man had nothing but one little ewe lamb, which he had bought. And he brought it up, and it grew up with him and with his children; it used to eat of his morsel, and drink from his cup, and lie in his bosom, and it was like a daughter to him. Now there came a traveler to the rich man, and he was unwilling to take one of his own flock or herd to prepare for the wayfarer who had come to him, but he took the poor man's lamb, and prepared it for the man who had come to him." Then David's anger was greatly kindled against the man; and he said to Nathan, "As Yahweh lives, the man who has done this deserves to die!"

David fails to understand the analogy until Nathan dramatically replies, "You are that man!" Then David repents, admits his guilt, and confesses his crime. Yahweh chooses to spare David's life, which perhaps comes as a surprise. If the law concerning adultery had been upheld to the letter, both David and Bathsheba would have been put to death. Moreover, David compounded one crime with a worse one, and it is difficult to imagine a more heinous case of marital infidelity. The writer takes it for granted that there is no one in the kingdom to punish David, but he can perceive divine displeasure with David in subsequent actions and experiences. The child conceived by his infidelity becomes sick and dies and David mourns deeply. It is Bathsheba's second child,

Solomon, who will eventually succeed his father as king of the united monarchy.

In fact, the punishment inflicted upon David does not end with the first child's death. For the Hebrew Bible's editor, David's crime of adultery is the turning point in his reign. Later rebellions and machinations all stem from this single event. In the following chapter (2 Samuel 13), David's eldest son, Amnon, sexually forces himself upon his half-sister Tamar, and then rejects her and a face-saving marriage. This event triggers a bloody consequence, as Tamar has a full brother, Absalom, who is not about to take Amnon's heinous act passively. He coldly waits two full years and then invites Amnon to a festival, gets him drunk, and orders his servants to kill him, thus avenging his sister.[9] Absalom then goes to stay with his grandparents in Geshur, and at last returns to make amends to his father. However, the tumultuous situation is never fully resolved. Shortly thereafter, Absalom leads a revolt against his father, which for a time forces David and much of his household to flee from Jerusalem. However, he does leave behind ten of his concubines to look after his palace. It is during this time that David is ironically punished for his earlier sin of adultery. While David is away from Jerusalem, Absalom enters the capital city and as part of his claim on his father's throne, he sets up a tent on the palace roof, for everyone to see, and has sexual relations with all ten of David's concubines, thus fulfilling Nathan's prophecy in 2 Samuel 12:11–12. Yahweh states that as part of the punishment for David's adultery,

> I will take your wives before your eyes, and give them to your neighbor, and he shall lie with your wives in the sight of this sun. For you did it secretly; but I will do this thing before all Israel, and before the sun.

And so David is punished tenfold for his action, and moreover, it is his own son who carries out the punishment. The penalties do not stop here for David, and Absalom does not go unpunished either in this theological account. Absalom's revolt ultimately ends in his own gruesome death, where he is left hanging by his hair from an oak tree with three darts in his heart and his body full of spear wounds.[10] Many years later, immediately prior to David's death, there is further contention for the throne, which results in the death of yet another son, Adonijah, this time by command of Solomon. The reader is made to believe that all this turmoil is a direct result of David's crime of adultery and subsequent murder of Uriah. While David's punishment may not have been the prescribed penalty of death for adulterers, Nathan's prophecy of rebuke immediately after his aforementioned parable certainly rings true. Nathan states that as punishment for killing Uriah by the sword of his enemy, "the sword shall never depart from your [David's] house."[11] So while David does not pay for his crime with his life, the consequential family turmoil he faces in many ways serves as a more severe punishment. David does not die a happy man.

We therefore have a clear violation of adultery—the eighth commandment, as enumerated in Jeremiah, in the eighth book of the Bible, the book of Samuel. Only one book remains before the close of the Primary History, and it is a great one.

The Ninth Commandment

You shall not bear false witness

The scarlet thread of commandment violations guiding us through the history of ancient Israel now nears its frayed and tattered end in exile. One book remains in the Primary History: the Book of Kings. Four centuries of history are recorded in the Book of Kings, and it is by no means a happy story. It opens with an elderly David's final days, spent in a vain attempt to prevent a civil war between his sons, and ends 560 B.C.E., twenty-six years after Jerusalem falls to the Babylonian army, and the nation is carried off into exile. Everything Israel had been working for is tragically taken away. The land promised to Abraham now lies more than five hundred miles to the west, as Israel dwells along the Tigris River. As we have seen, eight commandments have been violated in eight books. By now, it should come as a surprise to no one that the ninth commandment, which states, "You shall not bear false witness," is in fact clearly violated in the ninth and final book of the Primary History. Once again, the commandment is broken by the self-serving actions of an Israelite royal family, and once again, an innocent person loses his life.

The Book of Kings

The history recorded in Kings contains many of the most heinous tales in the Bible. As we mentioned, David's ongoing family problems are the subject of the book's opening chapters. As David lies in bed, weighed down by the effects of old age, the power of government inevitably slips from his grasp. He is losing power faster than he would like. Two of his sons are intent on becoming Israel's sole ruler. David had promised that Solomon, his son by Bathsheba, would succeed to the throne following his death. This decision did not sit well with Adonijah, David's fourth and eldest living son, who seized an opportunity to declare himself king even while his father remained alive. Adonijah's premature claim to the throne sends Bathsheba and the prophet Nathan to David's bedside, where they remind the aged David of his earlier promise and urge him to declare Solomon to be his rightful heir. Before David passes away, his choice of Solomon as successor is confirmed by the army and the people.

The tragedies inherent in the story above continue throughout the Book of Kings. One generation later, Solomon's son and heir Rehoboam foolishly alienates the majority of tribes, who split from the united monarchy in c. 922 B.C.E., forming a separate kingdom of Israel. For the next two hundred years, the ten northern tribes of Israel are governed by a variety of ruling houses in several capital cities, while the southern kingdom of Judah continues to be ruled by a descendant of David in Jerusalem. About eighty years after the dissolution of the united monarchy, Jehu carries out the bloodiest purge in the Bible, which results in the systematic murder of hundreds of people, including the kings of both Israel and Judah, and virtually all of their relatives. Moreover, the many atrocities in Kings go beyond the political sphere into the realm of religion. Israel's intimate relationship with Yahweh suffers when nearly all of the monarchs foster the worship of foreign deities. Yahweh's sovereignty and his laws are ignored time and time again despite the warnings of the prophets. Finally, the Assyrian empire destroys the northern kingdom of Israel in 722, and the southern kingdom of Judah meets a similar fate at the hands of the Babylonians in 586 B.C.E. As the Primary History comes to a close, the land promised by Yahweh to the descendants of Abraham is now lost, and the chosen people are held captive far away in Babylon. Psalm 137:1–6 masterfully captures the sorrow faced by the exilic community:

By the waters of Babylon, there we sat down and wept, when we remembered Zion. On the willows there we hung up our lyres. For there our captors required of us songs, and our tormentors, mirth, saying, "Sing us one of the songs of Zion." How shall we sing Yahweh's song in a foreign land? If I forget you, O Jerusalem, let my right hand wither. Let my tongue cleave to the roof of my mouth, if I do not remember you, if I do not set Jerusalem above my highest Joy.

The Book of Kings tells of countless deeds of wickedness, brutality, and terrible suffering. Nevertheless, out of all the atrocities committed in the Book of Kings, one sin stands out among the rest, and here we find a clear violation of the ninth commandment.

The Ninth Commandment: Bearing False Witness

The ninth commandment states: "You shall not bear false witness against your neighbor." Just what does this mean? Here the Hebrew Bible attempts to deal with a problem that has plagued justice from the very beginnings of human history: false testimony. The ninth commandment does not prohibit general lying, nor do any of the other commandments. However, all three parts of the Hebrew Bible, the Torah, the Prophets, and the Writings, speak forcefully about telling the truth. Deception is only permitted or encouraged to deceive the enemy or save life. But when one lies in a legal setting in an attempt to do harm to another person, this is when one "bears false witness," and this is when one breaks the ninth commandment.

False Witnesses Older Than Moses

Telling falsehoods in a legal setting has quite a long history of being unlawful. In fact, the Babylonian king Hammurapi, who composed a famous law code in the eighteenth century B.C.E. (more than five hundred years before Moses' birth!), saw this idea as so fundamentally important it became the very first law in his code.

***Hammurapi's Law Code (Eighteenth century B.C.E.). (Illustration courtesy of
the Louvre, Paris, France/Bridgeman Art Library.)***

Hammurapi's version says, "If a man accused a man, and
brought charge of murder against him, but has not proved it, his
accuser shall be put to death." The severity of the punishment indicates just how terrified the Babylonians were of false testimony.
The Israelites were also quite aware of the danger of this crime.

False testimony is also punished in the Hebrew Bible with a penalty quite similar to Hammurapi's code. Deuteronomy 19:16–21 prescribes that if a person wrongly accuses another, then the punishment for the alleged crime shall be applied to the accuser. That is to say, if one falsely accuses another of a crime that is punishable by death, then the accuser is put to death, and if one falsely accuses another of a lesser crime, then the lesser punishment is to be administered to the accuser. The Hebrew Bible also contends against the problem of false testimony by generally requiring two or more witnesses to convict a person of a crime.[1] However, there are ways of getting around this stipulation, as we shall see in our ninth commandment violation.

In order for us to meet with a clear case of commandment violation, we need to find a case of lying in a legal setting with intent to harm another person. If we only required general lying, the Hebrew Bible has many examples, beginning with Cain feigning ignorance of his dead brother's whereabouts.[2] Even many of the Bible's greatest heroes tell outright lies, including Isaac when he claims Rebekah is his sister,[3] as well as both Jacob and Rebekah when they deceive Isaac.[4] Also, Abraham is being half-honest when he says that Sarah is his sister, because Sarah is his half-sister.[5] Rahab lies to the King of Jericho's henchmen when she denies knowledge of the Israelite spies and their whereabouts.[6] Yet, not one of these cases involves lying in a legal setting. There is only one case in which a character in the Hebrew Bible bears false witness against a neighbor, and it involves the infamous couple Ahab and Jezebel.

Ahab, Jezebel, and Naboth's Vineyard

The terrible crime takes place in 1 Kings 21, and much like David's sin against Uriah, an innocent man loses his life because of the unfettered greed of a corrupt monarchy. The perpetrators this time are Ahab, the seventh king of Israel following the split into two kingdoms, and his Phoenician wife, Jezebel. Jezebel is a princess, daughter of the king of Tyre and Sidon (Phoenician coastal towns in modern Lebanon), and her marriage to Ahab

symbolizes the political alliance between Tyre and Sidon and Israel. When Jezebel comes to Israel, she brings her religion along
with her. The worship of the Phoenician deities Baal and Asherah
reaches unprecedented heights under Jezebel's rule as queen of Israel. Ahab builds an altar and temple for Baal in his capital city,
Samaria, sets up an Asherah, and is said to make Yahweh more angry than all the preceding kings of Israel.[7] Moreover, the Israelite
monarchy supports the 450 prophets of Baal and 400 prophets of
Asherah who gather on Mount Carmel to battle Elijah in the famous showdown between Baal and Yahweh in 1 Kings 18. Yahweh's great victory in providing fire for the prepared altar is
followed by the execution of Baal's prophets. When Jezebel hears
of her prophets' deaths, she seeks to deal the same fate to Elijah.
While it is clear that Jezebel fosters the worship of foreign deities,
the magnitude of this sin is perhaps small when compared to the
grievous crime she and her husband commit against an innocent
subject. The victim of this crime is Naboth, who, unfortunately
for him, happens to own a prime piece of real estate. Naboth has
inherited a vineyard, an ancestral property presumably owned by
his family since the conquest. But this vineyard adjoins the property of King Ahab, which also adds to the irony of this command
violation, as Ahab and Naboth *literally* are neighbors.

One day Ahab decides he wants to purchase the nearby land,
dig up the grapevines, and turn the property into a vegetable garden. Ahab makes Naboth an offer for his property, and even pro-
poses to provide another vineyard to replace the original, but to
Ahab's surprise, Naboth turns the offers down. Moreover, money
isn't the reason behind Naboth's declination. His reply to Ahab in
1 Kings 21:3 reveals his motivation: "Yahweh forbid that I should
give you the inheritance of my fathers." Exactly what is Naboth
referring to?

Realty and Jubilee:
Biblical Welfare Through Property Retention

Naboth's refusal to sell his inherited property stems from a remarkable law in Leviticus 25. Here Yahweh establishes a system of

property management, which ultimately reduces poverty and eliminates land monopolies and the enslavement of Israelite debtors. The focus of this system is the so-called *jubilee,* a special event that takes place every fifty years. During the jubilee year, all Israelite indentured slaves are released from servitude, and all property sold under financial burdens is returned to the original owner.[8] Consequently, despite Ahab's desires, Naboth is not suffering from "financial burdens," and he piously refuses to part with his family's ancestral land.

Ahab's Fit and Jezebel's Dire Response

Ahab is not pleased with Naboth's answer. After all, according to his title as king, he is the most powerful person in Israel, and ought to be shown more respect. But, rather than acting regally, Ahab returns to his palace to carry out one of the greatest pouting acts of all time. Not only does Ahab remain in bed all day with his face to the wall, but he refuses to eat as well.[9] His behavior is designed to attract the attention of his activist wife, to manipulate her to carry out a plan he does not want to carry out himself. Jezebel will not put up with her husband's childlike passivity, and she is quick to chastise the monarch. After all, she is used to a different kind of royal activity, having been raised in a Phoenician palace. And, Ahab is not otherwise noted for passivity. Prior to his fit he has been quite active in many realms, including politics, diplomacy, and the military. Rhetorically Jezebel asks her husband if he is not the ruler of Israel. Then she orders him to vacate the bed, arise, and begin eating again. Jezebel promises Israel's suddenly passive king that she will take care of everything.[10]

Jezebel then composes letters in the name of her husband, and commands that trumped-up charges of blasphemy and treason be brought against Naboth. Jezebel seals the letters with Ahab's signet and sends the letters to the civic administrators of Jezreel. As we mentioned before, according to biblical law, for a person to be convicted of charges as severe as those aimed at Naboth, two witnesses are required. But this law proves to be a small problem to someone with the resources of Jezebel. Sure enough, two men come forward in Jezreel claiming they both heard Naboth when he "cursed God and king."[11] There is nothing poor Naboth can do. He and his entire family are taken outside of the city and executed by a public stoning. Jezebel receives word that her plan has been carried out, and she informs Ahab, who promptly ceases pouting and heads outside to take possession of the land.[12]

This *karet* punishment is necessary for Jezebel's plan to work, as *karet* involves the forfeiture of property to the state. With a lesser crime Naboth's property would go to his children upon his death, whereas now it will go to the monarchy. Thus, Jezebel carefully chose the charge to be leveled against Naboth. (Roman and early European law had a similar punishment for treason. Under the laws of *lèse majesté,* or harming the ruler, forfeiture of property and attainder were automatic consequences for those convicted of treason.)

Not a Pleasant Way to Go

At the story's end, there is some justice in which one can take refuge. Ahab and Jezebel's action meets with severe repercussions. Just as Saul was supervised by the prophet Samuel, and Nathan watched over David's actions, Yahweh likewise checks the monarch's power in the reign of Ahab. The terrible sin committed by Ahab and Jezebel does not escape the watchful eye of the prophet Elijah. Yahweh promptly sends him to Ahab with a message: "In the place where dogs licked up the blood of Naboth, dogs will lick your own blood."[13] Furthermore, Yahweh has decided to take the throne away from Ahab for his crime against Naboth. Yet Ahab, like David, immediately repents his sin. For this Yahweh decides to postpone the loss of the kingship until the reign of Ahab's son, when the dynasty begun by Ahab's father, Omri, will come to an end.[14] Ahab is eventually killed in battle, where his blood spills all over his chariot. They bring the chariot back to the palace, and fulfilling the prophecy, dogs lick Ahab's blood in the same spot where Naboth was stoned.[15] Jezebel, although she lives longer than Ahab, meets an even more gruesome

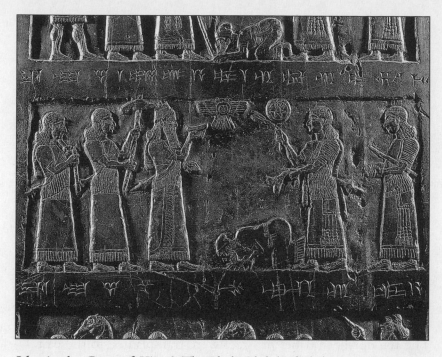

Jehu in the Court of Kings? The Black Obelisk of Shalmaneser III contains the only contemporary portrait of an Israelite monarch known to exist. On the larger obelisk, several kings are seen paying tribute to their Assyrian suzerain. Here, in one of its panels, a kin, named "Yaw, son of Omri," is believed by many scholars to be Jehu, the king anointed by Elijah. However, some think this may refer to Omri's grandson, Joram. (Illustration courtesy of Erich Lessing/Art Resource, N.Y.)

death. A usurper, Jehu, has slain her son, the king, and now has come after her.

She prepares to meet Jehu in her palace by applying makeup and dressing up, but it turns out to be all in vain because shortly thereafter three eunuchs throw her out a window, horses trample her dead body, dogs eat what is left, and her corpse thus becomes dung all over the field she was so intent on stealing for her husband.[16] And so the lesson from all this is that it is best not to testify falsely. As in David's securing others to commit murder (although the word is not used in the case of Uriah), so Jezebel acting for Ahab secures others to bear false witness. The crime is not perjury, as perjury requires lying under oath. In the Bible, witnesses are not put under oath. Jezebel's transgression is subornation. In any case, Ahab and Jezebel's sin against Naboth is a clear match to the ninth commandment, as they grievously bear false witness against their literal neighbor.

Israel continued to exist for more than one hundred years after Jezebel's death. Then, as the Assyrian army grew increasingly powerful, Hoshea, the final king of Israel, made a giant political blunder. Rather than continuing with a long tradition of paying tribute to the mighty Assyrian empire, he suddenly stopped payment and attempted to ally himself with the Egyptians. Shalmaneser V (reigned 726–722 B.C.E.), the Assyrian king, did not look kindly upon this action, and he brought his army west to the Israelite capital city of Samaria, capturing Hoshea and carrying him off in chains in 724 B.C.E. Shalmaneser V died before the captivity of the Israelite people, carried out by Sargon II in 722 B.C.E. The ten northern tribes of Israel were transplanted to the east.

The southern kingdom of Judah survived the Assyrian campaigns of both Shalmaneser V and Sargon II, who captured many of Judah's neighbors, but never invaded Judah. Then, in 701 B.C.E., Judah's luck changed with the campaign of Sennacherib, who surrounded Jerusalem with his forces and began the siege of Judah's capital city.

The events that then transpired vary depending on the source. According to 2 Kings 19:35–37 and Isaiah 37:36–37, an angel of Yahweh killed 185,000 of the Assyrian soldiers in their sleep. This miraculous turn of events forced Sennacherib to retreat to Nineveh. The Assyrians, of course, have a different version, known from the remarkable discovery of a cuneiform inscription known as Sennacherib's prism.

Denying divine intervention, the Assyrians claim the Judean king, Hezekiah, paid them a large sum of tribute, including thirty talents of gold (one talent equaled about sixty-six pounds) and eight hundred talents of silver, which the Bible also recounts, though the amounts differ.[17] The Assyrians, laden with treasures,

Jerusalem's Not So Fortunate Neighbors. These gruesome reliefs adorned the palace of Sennacherib in his capital city of Nineveh, and depict the Assyrian campaign of 701 B.C.E. when Lachish was besieged and subsequently captured. A horrible fate befell the residents of Lachish, where many were tortured and impaled. (Illustration courtesy of Erich Lessing/Art Resource, N.Y.)

then departed without destroying the city. The Greek historian Herodotus records yet another version. He claims that while the Assyrian soldiers were sleeping, a swarm of field mice devoured the soldiers' quivers, bows, and shield handles, forcing them the next day to flee unarmed.[18] Nevertheless, all three sources confirm that Hezekiah and Jerusalem narrowly escaped destruction, but they nevertheless survived. Thus Judah was granted a reprieve in contrast with Israel's annihilation. In fact, Judah outlasted even the

Sennacherib's Prism. *It is rare indeed when more than one source testifies to events that occurred in the ancient Near East. However, such is the case with Sennacherib's siege of Jerusalem, where not only the Bible but the Assyrian source exists as well. The Assyrian version is found on this prism discovered in 1920 on the floor of Sennacherib's palace in Nineveh. While the Hebrew Bible and the Assyrian version of the story differ on some issues, both agree that Jerusalem here escaped destruction. (Illustration courtesy of British Museum, London, U.K. / Bridgeman Art Library.)*

Assyrian empire's domination of the region. The dynasty begun by David lasted about 450 years, making it one of the longest in history.

But the bullet narrowly escaped during Hezekiah's reign hints at the changing structure of the ancient Near East. Both Egypt and Mesopotamia were growing increasingly stronger, and Judah's location between their empires created a difficult if not impossible situation for Judean rulers. When they allied with Egypt, as Hezekiah had done, the Assyrians invaded and forced them to change their loyalties. When Judean monarchs vassalized under Mesopotamia, the Egyptians forcefully pressured them to reconsider. The complexity of the political situation can be seen in the story surrounding the death of Josiah, Hezekiah's great-grandson and reputedly the greatest king of the Bible. According to 2 Kings 23:25:

> Before him there was no king like him, who turned to Yahweh with all his heart and with all his soul and with all his might, according to all the laws of Moses. And after him did not arise any like him.

Josiah came to the throne at the age of eight and in 621 B.C.E., the eighteenth year of his reign, he instituted the greatest religious reforms in the history of the Judean monarchy.[19] The finding of a very important scroll inside the Jerusalem Temple precipitated the reforms.[20] This scroll appears to have contained the majority of the Book of Deuteronomy. Josiah had his scribe read the book aloud, and upon hearing its words, Josiah tore his clothes in shame and stated, "Great is Yahweh's anger that is burning against us, because our fathers have not obeyed the words of this book, to do according to all that is written concerning us."[21] Josiah then embarked on a process of unprecedented religious centralization. From the Jerusalem Temple, he removed an Asherah and many other items sanctioned for gods other than Yahweh. He reinstituted the holiday of Passover, so his subjects made a vernal pilgrimage to Jerusalem to commemorate the avoidance of the final plague (the death of the firstborn), and to celebrate the Exodus. Josiah's reform transcended Jerusalem, as he destroyed sanctuaries and places of worship throughout Judea. Even Israel to the north, part of Assyria's empire, was rid of shrines. The cleansing was only possible because Assyria's neighbor to the south, Babylon, was rapidly gaining in power, and Assyria herself entered a turbulent period of civil war. Assyria's former vassals were thus provided an opportunity for greater independence, and Josiah seized the opportunity to implement his reform.

But then, in 609 B.C.E., Josiah was shot dead with an Egyptian arrow at Megiddo. His death was cataclysmic to the extent that now many believe the site of Megiddo will be intimately connected with the world's end. (The term Armageddon comes from the Hebrew *har megiddo,* with *har* meaning "mountain.") Josiah's death, along with a famous battle in 1479 B.C.E. between Thutmose III and a coalition of Canaanite forces, indelibly links Megiddo with warfare. Thus Revelation 16:16 claims Armageddon (Mount Megiddo) will be the site of an apocalyptic battle.[22] The reasons behind the engagement between Josiah's forces and the Egyptians were unexpected, because the Egyptians had come to Megiddo on their way to assist their time-honored nemesis, the Assyrians. In the bizarre world of ancient Near Eastern politics, the Egyptians had grown fearful of the Babylonians' abrupt rise, and so decided that backing a weakening Assyria would best serve their interest by creating a Mesopotamian balance of power. It is unclear whether Josiah's motivations were to halt the Egyptian march to ensure the Assyrian demise, or whether some other factors were involved. But the circumstances of his death vividly illustrate the tumultuous nature of Judah's location, wedged between powerful empires of Egypt and Mesopotamia.

Only four kings reigned after Josiah. Three of them were his sons, one his grandson. Josiah's son and immediate successor was Jehoahaz, but he reigned only three months before Pharaoh Neco removed him to Egypt, where he remained in captivity until his death. Neco placed another of Josiah's sons, Jehoiakim, on the throne. Initially a vassal of Egypt, Jehoiakim was forced to change political alliances when the Babylonian army under King Nebuchadnezzar invaded Judah.[23] Thereafter, Jehoiakim paid tribute to Babylon for three years, and then rebelled. He died just before facing Babylonian reprisal, which fell on his son Jehoiachin, Josiah's grandson, who inherited a soon-to-be besieged capital city of Jerusalem.

This time Jerusalem's walls are breached, Yahweh's Temple is looted, and Jehoiachin is taken away in chains to Babylon.[24] Nebuchadnezzar now places Zedekiah, Josiah's third son, on the throne. Zedekiah, like his predecessors, rebels against Babylon, clearly an unwise move in retrospect. King Nebuchadnezzar returns along with the Babylonian army and again lays siege to Jerusalem. The city falls in 586 B.C.E., and the patience of Nebuchadnezzar has been exhausted. The chief priests and other officials are executed.[25] Zedekiah is captured, and he is forced to watch as every one of his sons is put to death, and then his eyes are put out, so that the slaughter of his children is the final thing he sees.[26] Yahweh's Temple, which has stood for four hundred years, is burnt to the ground, along with the royal palace and other residences.[27] The Judeans now meet a fate similar to that suffered by their northern kindred 136 years earlier. They are forced into exile in Mesopotamia.

The Primary History comes to an end with the Promised Land lost, and while it is not a happy ending by any means, the final chapter ends with a glimpse of hope for the fate of the Israelites. We are informed that Jehoiachin, the former king of Judah and a descendant of David, remains alive in captivity in Babylon. He had been dethroned and taken into captivity in 597 B.C.E. for revolting. But now, because the Babylonian king has taken a liking to him, Jehoiachin is doing pretty well.[28]

The Primary History ends here. It was written for the Exiles to explain the past, influence the present, and give hope for the future, although they will have to learn to obey the commandments if there is to be a future. While the Primary History ends here, we know from Ezra-Nehemiah, a later historical book within the Hebrew Bible, that within fifty years following the destruction of Jerusalem, the first group of Israelites returns under the leadership of Sheshbazzar c. 538 B.C.E. The name resembles

Shenazzar, one of the sons of Jehoiachin, but the identification is not certain. A second wave of returnees is led by Zerubbabel, the son of Shealtiel, another of Jehoiachin's sons. Zerubbabel is credited with the rebuilding of the Temple in 521–515 B.C.E. So the glimmer of hope placed at the conclusion of the Primary History does end up being realized.

The Israelites have suffered greatly for their sins, although as we have seen, these sins were no minor transgressions. Yahweh's Chosen People have violated in order the first nine of Yahweh's most hallowed laws. Now they realize that their punishment is due to violating Yahweh's most sacred commandments, and that if they one day return to the Promised Land, they must keep these laws. But now we are out of books in the Primary History, and as every child learns in Sunday school, there are Ten Commandments. To find out how the tenth commandment fits into our model, let us turn to the final chapter.

The Tenth Commandment?

You shall not covet

nd so, as the nine books of the Primary History ended in the last chapter, and as there are ten commandments, just where do we put the remaining one? Before we address this dilemma and bring our study to a close, one last point of variation must be discussed: the wording of the tenth commandment. The variations may give us a possible clue as to where the tenth commandment fits in our model.

Three Differences in a Command Presentation

As I discussed briefly at the beginning of this journey, there are three major differences in the tenth commandment as it appears in Exodus 20 and Deuteronomy 5.

Exodus 20:17	Deuteronomy 5:18
You shall not **covet** your neighbor's house; you shall not **covet** your neighbor's wife, or his male servant, or his female servant, or his ox, or his donkey, or anything that belongs to your neighbor.	And you shall not **covet** your neighbor's wife; and you shall not **desire** your neighbor's house, his field, or his male servant, or his female servant, his ox, or his donkey, or anything that belongs to your neighbor.

The first variation, in word order, has been the subject of some discussion. While the coveted objects prohibited in Exodus begin with "house" followed by "wife," Deuteronomy places "wife" first, then "house." Some have argued the reading in Exodus is thus more misogynist, claiming that putting "wife" after "house" demotes her to a household possession on the same level as the slaves and livestock that follow. However, this is simply not the case. The Hebrew word "house" extends well beyond the physical house, and can mean not only possessions but also family. When descendants of King David claim to be from the "house of David," they are not stating that David owns them, but rather that they are part of his family. Moreover, there is no evidence that the list of items presented in both accounts proceeds from the most valuable to the least. The word order simply varies, and there is not much more one can safely say regarding the significance of that. The other two differences are much less controversial. The commandment in Exodus uses the verb "covet" *(tachmod)* two times, while in Deuteronomy the second occurrence is replaced with "desire" *(titavveh)*. Because these two Hebrew words are synonyms, not much significance can be found in the variation. However, the third variation is interesting, as it calls our attention to this final commandment's purpose. The tenth commandment in Deuteronomy 5:21 adds among the items not to be coveted the word *field*. This could be a case of haplography, where the scribe of Exodus 20's eye missed "field" and jumped to the next word "manservant." Both the Septuagint of Exodus 20:17 and the Nash papyrus have the word *field*. Another possibility is that the variation is intentional. In either case, the inclusion of the word *field* with the items not to be coveted seems to indicate just how this unique tenth commandment fits into our model, as we shall soon see.

Actions Speak Louder

While the prohibition against coveting your neighbor's property does not match a specific story of commandment violation, it definitely fits into our model, but not in the same fashion as the previous nine commandments. The tenth commandment is of a very different nature from the previous nine in that it deals with *motivation* rather than *action*. Having other gods before Yahweh, making graven images, taking God's name in vain, not observing the Sabbath, dishonoring your parents, theft, murder, adultery, and false witness all involve illicit actions on the part of the perpetrator. Now, the tenth commandment does not speak of action, but rather for the first time forbids an attitude. In modern and ancient courtrooms, the underlying attitude or intent of a perpetrator is vitally important and punishable but *after* the crime is committed, never before. Just as a person's attitude cannot be punished in the court of a modern civilized country in the absence of a criminal action, neither could he be held accountable for his attitude in the courts of ancient Israel. To break the tenth commandment is in violation of God's will, but it is not in violation of Israelite law. It is therefore not surprising that no definite example exists in the Primary History where the tenth commandment is linked to a particular episode, as we find in the previous nine commandments. But then, what purpose does it serve?

The Tenth Commandment and the Seven Deadly Sins

The tenth commandment is a supplement to the previous commandments. It presents the motivations behind the crimes, especially for violations of commandments six through nine. When Achan steals the booty from Jericho, his crime occurs only after he acts upon his desires. The same can be said for the inhabitants of Gibeah, who covet the Levite guest of their neighbor, and wind up brutally raping his concubine to death. David likewise covets, and the crime occurs when he acts upon this motivation and has sexual relations with his neighbor's wife. Jesus discusses coveting in his Sermon on the Mount, when he says that when one looks upon a married woman lustfully, he has already committed adultery in his heart.[1] Thus, according to both the Decalogue and the Sermon on the Mount, David sins against God when he covets the wife of Uriah, but he commits adultery only after consummating his sexual relationship with Bathsheba. In much the same fashion, Ahab violated the ninth commandment. His desire for his neighbor's property is not a punishable offense. It is only after he and Jezebel act upon their coveting and bring trumped-up charges against Naboth that they break biblical law. Moreover, just as David's sin violated two commandments (adultery and murder), and Ahab and Jezebel's crime broke two (false witness and murder), so the tenth commandment is directly involved in all four of the preceding regulations. Thus, the tenth commandment does not find a specific violation, because it is not like the previous nine. It provides the underlying motivation for each of the criminal violations in numbers six through nine.

Similar in nature to the tenth commandment is the warning against the Seven Deadly Sins, one of which is Coveting. The Seven Deadly Sins are sins against the Law of God, but they are not crimes punishable by the state. Coveting, along with Greed, Pride, Envy, Sloth, Anger, and Lust all lead to crimes and punishments, but in themselves are not accountable or punishable as crimes. Buddhism maintains a similar tenet. The Buddha's observation that all suffering arises from desire is quite similar to the tenth commandment. If one can adhere to the tenth commandment, and not covet, then the chance of breaking commandments six through nine is eliminated.

The nature of the tenth commandment is further clarified by an understanding of the fifth commandment, to honor one's parents. Just as the tenth commandment controls or governs the preceding four (six through nine), so the fifth commandment is linked to its preceding laws (one through four). Adherence to the first four commandments necessitates parental obedience. This is why Moses instructs the people to learn the commandments:

You shall teach them to your children, and you shall speak of them when you sit in your house, and when you walk on the road, and when you lie down, and when you rise.

DEUTERONOMY 6:7

In fact, throughout Deuteronomy 5 and 6, Moses implores the parents to teach the children to obey God, to perpetually "love Yahweh your God with all your heart, and with all your soul, and with all your might" (Deuteronomy 6:5). Parents, not kings or law courts, will convey the first four commandments to their children—this is why honoring parents is so vital. Additionally, the Book of Deuteronomy is the pivot of the Primary History, the halfway point and the transition from wanderings and Moses to settlement and Joshua. So too is the fifth commandment a pivot of the nine commandments. In practice it would be the prime rule of life, a law which necessitates compliance with all other commandments.

Two Clues and One Conclusion

Two clues confirm the prohibition against coveting as a supplement to commandments six through nine. The first clue can be found in Joshua 7:21. When Achan confesses to his crime of violating the sixth commandment by stealing the spoils from Jericho, he claims that after seeing the items, "I coveted them." Here we find the exact Hebrew root used in the tenth commandment *(chamad)*. Thus the tenth commandment clearly provides the impetus for Achan's crime, as Achan himself acknowledges. The second clue exists in the aforementioned addition of the word *field* to the tenth commandment as recorded in Deuteronomy. It should be remembered that in the previous chapter, Ahab coveted a "vineyard," a word frequently parallel to field.[2] Thus we seem to have two bookends in the stories recording the violations of commandments six and nine, which mirror the tenth commandment's language, highlighting the tenth commandment's relevancy as a motivation behind the sins beginning with Joshua's tale of theft, and ending with Kings' story of bearing false witness.

The case can be made that there is only one change in the Primary History from the standard order of the commandments listed in Exodus 20 and Deuteronomy 5: the eighth commandment, prohibiting theft, has been moved to number six to accommodate the story as recorded in the Primary History. The other commandments and books are in the same sequence, so the change is slight. Both this new order and the standard order own a great deal of symmetry. In our order, commandments six (theft) and seven (murder) are premonarchic and involve the Tribal Confederacy, while eight (adultery) through nine (false witness) are monarchic and involve kings. In the order as manifested in Exodus 20 and Deuteronomy 5, the violations of commandment six (murder) and seven (adultery) involve illegal sex and murder, i.e., persons. The breach of eight (theft) and nine (false witness) involve theft of property, divine and divinely ordained. But despite the order, all four of the violations are governed by greed.

Conclusion

◆━◆✕◆━◆

The End of Our Journey

The Primary History (Genesis through Kings) tells the story of the nation of Israel. The founding father of the nation is the patriarch Abraham, with whom God seals a covenant by oath. This oath embodies a promise—unilateral, unconditional, and irrevocable—that Israel shall have posterity and property (i.e., the Promised Land) and shall serve as a role-model, the means or agent of blessing to the nations of the world.[1] That covenant of divine commitment is progressively and increasingly fulfilled in the long narrative that follows. The process is initiated by Abraham himself with his migration to the land of Canaan, his march through the length and breadth of the country to be settled by his descendants, as well as his fateful journey to and return from Egypt, which prefigures the sojourn in and exodus from that "house of bondage";[2] and near the end of his life, the emblematic purchase of the cave of Machpelah as the burial place for him and his family (the first long-term acquisition on record).[3]

The complex, tortuous experience winds its way through the books of the Torah and the Former Prophets, reaching a successful climax with the conquest and settlement of the land: the East Bank of the Jordan under the leadership of Moses, while the West Bank (the heartland of Israel) was captured by his successor, Joshua. Although the biblical language tends to be exuberant and extravagant, the reality emerges in time: the

Conquest was incomplete, with sizable tracts remaining in the hands of the former occupants, and ephemeral, with neighboring enemies exerting and exercising authority over the Israelite inhabitants for extended periods. After continuing struggles with recalcitrant and hostile neighbors, the ancient promise is fully realized with the accession of David and his stunning military victories, which culminate in the formation of Greater Israel, filling the territory between Egypt to the southwest and Assyria to the northeast.

The United Kingdom of David and Solomon is celebrated as the apogee of Israel's historical adventure and the fulfillment of the divine commitment to the patriarchs at the end of the Book of Samuel (David) and the early part of the Book of Kings (Solomon).

The Covenant of Human Obligation

Alongside the story of the patriarchal covenant of divine commitment runs that of the covenant of human obligation. This covenant, which is proclaimed by God through Moses, and ratified by the people of Israel at Mount Sinai (Mount Horeb in the Deuteronomic tradition) conforms in large part to the standard suzerainty treaties of the ancient Near East (also called suzerain-vassal treaties as described in chapter 3). However, Israel's covenant is unique in that it is made with a divine suzerain, and it spells out the obligations of the human party to its divine overlord.

The essential content, terms, and obligations imposed on Israel consists of the Ten Commandments, preserved in two equivalent forms in Exodus 20 and Deuteronomy 5. The message and meaning of the covenant are that as Yahweh the God of Israel continues to fulfill the promises made to the Fathers, by bringing the Israelites out of bondage in Egypt (already accomplished) and with the assurance that he will also bring them to the land of Canaan and give them possession of it, so they in turn must strictly obey the stipulations laid down in the Decalogue, specific instructions scattered in the different law codes and manuals of the Torah.

Conforming to the rules and regulations will ensure both the survival and success of the nation and the fulfillment of the remaining promises, as well as the continuing possession of the land and endless peace and prosperity for the inhabitants of this kingdom of God.

At the same time, failure to uphold their side of the bargain, failure to obey and perform the commandments will result in dire consequences, and as with individual violators, the nation itself will perish. The combination of promise and threat is presented in eloquent sermons by Moses in the farewell addresses recorded in the Book of Deuteronomy, which unite the two covenants on which the narrative hangs and proceeds to its inevitable conclusion.[4] We have twin narratives of divine promise and fulfillment on the one hand, and human obligation and violation on the other, the one beginning with Abraham in Genesis and reaching a climax with the establishment of the United Kingdom of Israel under David and Solomon. The other is set in motion in Exodus with the mediation of the covenant of human obligation by Moses. It continues to the very end with the demise of the nation, including the burning and razing of the Temple of Yahweh, erected by Solomon almost four hundred years earlier, a crowning dynastic achievement symbolizing and coinciding with the fullest realization of the promises made to the patriarchs.

The Rise and Fall of Israel

In this book, we have been concerned primarily with the covenant ratified at Mount Sinai, the covenant mediated by Moses, by which the people bound themselves to worship and serve Yahweh alone, and obey without exception the laws laid down in the Decalogue and expanded and elaborated elsewhere in the traditions recorded in the Torah. The story of what happened in and to Israel after the giving of the law and the ratification of the covenant (Exodus 19–24) is told successively in the major components of the Primary History. The story is complex and varied, with the ups and downs that any small nation (even the United Kingdom at its greatest extent was modest or medium-sized at best by ancient standards) experienced in an era of constant upheaval. Despite the rise and fall of empires, vast social and economic changes, and political and diplomatic shifts, the underlying theme and overarching framework are the covenant relationship between the God of the universe and his chosen people. The central emphasis is on the historical outcome as the result of the persistent rebellion against the divine overlord, of continuous violations of the terms of that agreement on the part of the vassal community, Israel. Israel's rebellion is articulated by the frequent repetition of the formula of the first commandment: they have abandoned Yahweh their God to follow other gods, themselves mere idols, bowing down to them and serving them.[5] All of the sins and crimes are consolidated into a gross violation of the first two commandments, which are seen as the basic and ultimate obligation of the people, whose rampant repudiation of this requirement is seen as symbolic of the full-scale rebellion against the rule of God and total abandonment by Israel of its solemnly sworn commitment to worship and serve Yahweh alone and to obey all of his laws.

The above analysis and interpretation of Israelite history are expounded at length in the commentary on the fall of Samaria, the capital city of the northern kingdom in 722 B.C.E., and explain in some detail how and why this irreversible disaster occurred. In the end, it was not just the fortunes or misfortunes of armed conflict that brought about disaster, or the unquestionable fact that the Assyrian armed forces were larger, better equipped, and more effective than those of Israel or any or all of its allies, it was the fact that Yahweh, the all-powerful deity, was punishing his own people for breaking the covenant. We quote from 2 Kings 7:5–17:

> The king of Assyria [Shalmanezer V] went up against the whole land; and he attacked Samaria and he besieged it for three years (724–722 B.C.E.) In the ninth year of Hoshea [the king of Israel], the king of Assyria captured Samaria and exiled Israel to Assyria. And he settled them in Helah

and on the Habor, the river of Gozan, and the cities of the Medes. So it happened because the Israelites sinned against Yahweh their God, the one who brought them up from the land of Egypt, from under the hand of Pharaoh, the king of Egypt, and they revered other gods. And they walked in the statutes of the nations that Yahweh had dispossessed from the presence of the Israelites . . . and the Israelites proclaimed statements, which were not true, about Yahweh their God; and they built for themselves high places in all of their cities from watchtower to fortified city. And they set up pillars and Asherim on every high hill and under every leafy tree. And they offered up burnt offerings there, at all the high places, like the nations that Yahweh had driven into exile from their presence. And they did terrible things to provoke Yahweh. And they served the idols, concerning which Yahweh had said to them: "You shall not make this thing." And Yahweh testified against Israel and against Judah by the hand of every prophet and every seer, saying: "Turn from your wicked ways and keep my commandments and my statutes, according to the whole Torah that I commanded your fathers and that I delivered to you by the hand of my servants the prophets. But they did not listen, and they hardened their neck, like the neck of their fathers, who did not have faith in Yahweh their God. And they spurned his statutes and his covenant, the one that he cut with their fathers, and his testimonies, which he testified against them. And they walked after The Nothing and they became nothing, and after the nations that surrounded them, concerning whom Yahweh had commanded them not to behave as they did. And they abandoned all the commandments of Yahweh their God, and they made for themselves a graven image ["two calves"], and they made "Asherah" and they prostrated themselves before the whole host of heaven, and they served Baal. And they made their sons and their daughters pass through the fire, and they performed sorceries and practiced divination; and they sold themselves to do the evil in the sight of Yahweh to provoke him. And Yahweh became extremely angry at Israel, and he removed them from his presence. None was left except for the tribe of Judah by itself. Judah also did not keep the commandments of Yahweh their God, and they walked in the statutes of Israel, just as the latter did. So Yahweh rejected the whole seed of Israel, and he afflicted them and delivered them into the hand of marauders, until he had hurled them out of his presence . . .

The same line of reasoning would be applied to Judah, details changing only here and there. One hundred and thirty-five years later, the same fate would overtake the southern kingdom, only this time it would be the Babylonians rather than the Assyrians who would administer the divine sanctions and the fatal blows to national existence, and different images would be condemned, instead of the calves associated with the north's idolatry. While it is important and not difficult to establish the general plan and tenor of the Deuteronomic History and the Primary History as the story of the making and breaking of the Sinai/Horeb covenant and the dire consequences of such defection, I have argued for the possibility that there was much more to this pattern in the correlation of the books of the Primary History and the commandments of the Decalogue. The correspondence between books and commandments was more precise: one for one and in the order in which the books and the commandments occur in the Hebrew Bible. If my argument is correct, it shows that the final redaction of the whole work was based on a master plan with a visible internal structure to which the full narrative, with all of its colorful details, is tied. It also shows that the whole work, almost exactly half of the Hebrew Bible, was the end product of single mind or compiler (or a very small committee, like the one that produced the famous King James Version of the Bible).

Exceptions to the Rule

The correspondence between command violations and books of the Bible is impressive, and the connections seem quite certain. Yet, three possible exceptions require explanation and deserve to be considered directly: one each at the beginning, middle, and end.

As for the order of the commandments, we followed the list in the Decalogue as found in Exodus 20 and Deuteronomy 5: the order and the summary statement is the same in both cases, the differences occurring in the added comments. The order of the commandments as I have derived them from the narratives in the books of the Primary History conforms to the order in the decalogues, with a single exception. Numbers six, seven, and eight in the decalogues come out as numbers eight, six, and seven in the narratives or books of the Primary History. The only change needed to make the lists conform is to move number eight (that is, the sixth in the narratives) two places back, after number seven. The fact that eight of the nine commandments are in the same order in both lists (of the narratives as we have compiled the list, and the decalogues as recorded in Exodus and Deuteronomy) carries us far beyond the boundary of chance or random selection. Moreover, it is precisely those three commandments (numbers six through eight in the decalogues) that we have seen turn up in different arrangements in ancient lists: e.g., the Septuagint and New Testament. So it is fair to say that the order in the narratives was deliberately modeled on that of the decalogues.

The first possible (but not actual) anomaly derives from the fact that the Sinai/Horeb covenant was not promulgated and ratified until the Book of Exodus. So we cannot begin the countdown of violations with the Book of Genesis; we must begin with Exodus and only after the ratification of the covenant. It is in Exodus that we find the first convincing violation of the first and second commandments—in fact, within forty days of the ratification rite. The double violation described in Exodus 32 corresponds very closely to the way in which the two commandments are listed and combined in the formal statements in Exodus 20:3–5 and Deuteronomy 5:7–10.

Thus apostasy and idolatry were originally distinct proscribed actions: apostasy was defined as having other gods, i.e., worshiping and serving them, while idolatry referred to the making of an image of Yahweh in any form; images of other gods were already ruled out by the first commandment. In time, however, the commandments were blended into each other, and apostasy and idolatry were practically indistinguishable. The worship of any god other than Yahweh was a form of idolatry as well as apostasy, since other gods were defined as idols, empty things, and any image, once images of Yahweh had been forbidden and destroyed, was that of another god. In the course of time, then, the second commandment was regarded as a special case or reinforcement of the first, and grammatically and syntactically was incorporated into the first, with the comment in the next verse being applied equally to both. The generalizing admonition at the end of the second commandment that "You shall not bow before them and you shall not serve (be enslaved) to them . . ." refers back to the other gods mentioned in the first commandment, but encompasses the idols of the second commandment as well.

This analysis finds support in the practice in both Judaism and in major Christian communities (e.g., Roman Catholics, Lutherans, and Anglicans) to put these commandments together.[6] Nevertheless, there can be little doubt that originally, these were separate commandments, dealing with different aspects or features of the worship and service of Yahweh, the only true God. On the one hand, Israel must be faithful to Yahweh alone and have no other gods at all, for any reason or purpose. On the other hand, Israel must not make any images of any kind, whether representing Yahweh or any other god.

At the other end of the Decalogue, we have the problem of the Tenth Commandment, for which we do not have a corresponding book in the Primary History and for which there is no single story of explicit violation. The position we have taken is that the Tenth Commandment is different in basic structure from all of the others in that it focuses attention on an attitude or state of mind, rather than on an action or speech as the others do. Simply put, coveting is a sin but not a punishable crime, although it is often causally linked with a very serious offense, capital crimes. We have argued that coveting provides the motivation, underlying cause, and driving force behind the offenses listed in the second table (listed on page 98): numbers six through nine in the Decalogue. In each of these, coveting supplies the motivating power that leads to the commission of the capital crime and the violation of the covenant. Coveting is defined more precisely as "greed" in the stories for numbers six and nine in our listing: in Joshua 6–7, the story of Achan and his theft of the sacred booty from the fall of Jericho; and in 1 Kings 21, the story of Ahab and Jezebel and the expropriation of Naboth's vineyard. In the other two cases, the qualifying term is "lust," as described in numbers seven and eight: in Judges 19–21 the story of the rape of the Levite's concubine and in 2 Samuel 11–12, the story of David's adultery with Bathsheba, the wife and later widow of Uriah. So the tenth commandment is incorporated into the second table (see page 98) along with the four violations in which coveting is directly involved as the motivating force in the commission of the crimes. (Compare 1 Timothy 6:10: "For the *love* of money is the root of all evils.")

The third anomaly is to be found in the sequence of numbers six, seven, and eight, in which the order is different in the narrative from that of the decalogues in Exodus 20 and Deuteronomy 5. There are two considerations here. The first is that it is precisely these three commandments that are found arranged differently in various places in both the Hebrew and Greek Bibles (including the New Testament).[7] It is not difficult to imagine why the order was subject to change in the course of transmission, whether orally or in writing. One reason is that these commandments are the shortest ones of all, consisting of only two words each in the original Hebrew. The first one, the negative particle *(lo')* is the same in all three, and the following verb begins with the same letter in all cases (t = second person masculine singular pronoun, "you": *tirtsach, tena'ep*, and *tignov*). In the process of repeating them or copying them, it would be easy to change the order and, in fact, this has happened in various recensions of the Bible. Curiously, as we have pointed out, the order that we have found in the narratives of the Primary History corresponds to the order pronounced by Jeremiah in famous Temple speech, which is epitomized in Jeremiah 7:8, presumably recorded and reported by his faithful scribe, Baruch.

Since, on many grounds, the same Baruch is a leading candidate as one (if not the last) of the Deuteronomic Historians, the correspondence in the order of the commandments between the Deuteronomic History (in the narratives themselves) and the order in Jeremiah 7 is of special interest. This correspondence could lead to the view that the sequence in the narrative finds support in the order that Jeremiah used and presumably regarded as authoritative in his day, even if it disagreed with the official order in the canonical decalogues in Exodus 20 and Deuteronomy 5.

Who Is Responsible for This Scarlet Thread?

We suggested at the outset of our journey that the presence of a scarlet thread of sin, that is, the correlation of the commandments and the stories illustrating their violations in the Primary History, reveals the hand of a Master Editor or Redactor, a person commonly designated "R" (for "Redactor") by modern scholars, an individual who is anonymous to us, but certainly a real person with a name and a calling, who richly deserves the honor of recognition for compiling and producing the first full-scale history of a nation, a person who preceded Herodotus, the so-called "Father of History," by at least a century. In fact, it is at least possible that the latter was acquainted with the work of the former and modeled his own justly famous *History of the Persian War* upon it.[8]

A Balanced Book

The key to understanding *why* this Editor would accept and implement an alternate order of command violations may be connected to the idea of "pairing." A frequently decisive literary device in demonstrating overall planning and execution is "pairing" or what we may call "symmetry." Symmetry can be seen in the largest parts of the Bible: the Primary History, the longest single narrative in the whole Hebrew Bible, constitutes almost exactly 50 percent of the Hebrew Bible. It is balanced by the latter two parts: the Latter Prophets, which match the Former Prophets, and the Writings, which match the Torah, in an inverted or chiastic relationship (i.e., Torah + Former Prophets // Latter Prophets + Writings); at the same time, discrete pairs, especially in the parallelism that dominates Hebrew poetry, are almost ubiquitous.[9] An example from the very beginning of the Book of Genesis will illustrate the use of this technique in order to demonstrate symmetry, which in turn reflects planning, completeness, totality, and perfection.

In the very beginning of the Bible, eight acts of Creation are distributed among the first six days of the first week, with the seventh day reserved for passive rest. On the face of it, this does not look like a promising organization, but the writer/compiler is up to the task. Thus there is one act of creation on each of the first two days, and two on the third day. Matching that pattern, there is one act on each of the next two days (the fourth and fifth), and two more acts on the sixth day, bringing the work to completion, and in a form of bilateral symmetry, the simplest and most efficient kind. There are corresponding links between the acts on the first and fourth days, and on the second and fifth days, to show that the creator (small "c") could spin more elaborate patterns while presenting the more simple one in the foreground. So it is with the arrangement and distribution of the commandments within the Decalogue itself, and across the whole fabric of the Primary History.

Reverting to the Hebrew Bible as a whole, we noted that the Primary History, consisting of two major parts (Torah + Former Prophets) is matched by the second half of the Prophetic Corpus (Latter Prophets + the Writings, a catchall of the remaining books). In the present Hebrew Bible the numerical sequence is also symmetrical: thus, Torah (five books) + Prophets (eight books but divided: four Former Prophets + four Latter Prophets) + Writings (eleven books) = twenty-four books, itself a multiple divisible, representing totality and perfection. (It is the number of books in the great Greek canonical epics by Homer, and corresponds exactly to the number of letters in the Greek alphabet, the alphabet itself being a symbol of totality and infinity.) We are justified, therefore, in looking for similar structural features and symmetrical devices in the enumeration and distribution of the Commandments in the Decalogue in the course of the narratives dealing with them in the Primary History.

Accomplices in Crime

Pairing is the most common and frequent device in the arrangement of the commandments and the stories about them in the Primary History. We have already discussed the first two, which are associated with the single episode of the golden calf. In a single action, the Israelites commit both apostasy and idolatry, according to the description and the charges in the story itself. And, as we have also seen, this pairing is strengthened by the blending and merging of the two commandments in the Protestant and Catholic traditions into a single statement in the Jewish tradition.

The next pair, numbers three and four, also constitute a pair. Just as the story of the first pair takes place at Sinai where the Decalogue was first proclaimed and ratified shortly thereafter, so the next two stories take place in the wilderness under similar circumstances. The accounts follow a common outline and derive from the same literary source (P = Priestly Document). Both stories are told briefly and the same major point is made: violations of the terms of the covenant between God and Israel, especially those recorded in the Decalogue, which are representative of the basic bond between the suzerain overlord and his vassal people, are capital offenses and must be dealt with rigorously by the people as a whole through their chosen leaders. All adults must participate in rendering judgment: witnesses to the offense must testify and the whole adult population must have a hand (literally) in administering the punishment. Only by being agents of retributive justice can the people be exonerated from collective guilt and be exempted from collective punishment for such violations.

In each case, an unnamed man breaks the relevant commandment: in the first instance, by cursing God (blasphemy, which is prohibited by the third commandment, although the latter is stated much more broadly and would include many other instances of the misuse of the name of God, as in lying under oath). While the initial or primary focus of the commandment may well have been in regard to involving the divine name to confirm a statement known to be false by the person making the oath, it would also and certainly cover the matter of blasphemy, understood to be cursing God himself. That this was a live issue in classical Israel is shown by various formulations and examples in the Bible.

The explicit prohibition is found in the Book of the Covenant,[10] which belongs to the oldest stratum of legal documents in the Bible.[11] A specific example is discussed at some length in this book—the case of Naboth's Vineyard. In this story, an innocent man (Naboth) is falsely charged with the crime of cursing God and king, and he is punished under the terms of the covenant not only with execution but with the extirpation *(karet)* of his family. We have also discussed the matter found in the Book of Job, where this issue of "cursing God" comes up in a different context. Job fears that his children may curse God in their hearts,[12] while The Satan is confident that when Job has suffered sufficiently he will "curse God to His face."[13] Later Job's wife joins the chorus: "Curse God and die!"[14]

In the matching case, an unnamed man gathers wood on the Sabbath, a clear if seemingly harmless violation of the fourth commandment. In this case as in the previous one, this unnamed man is arrested and inquiry is made through Moses about the appropriate legal process and the administration of the requisite punishment for this breach of the covenant with God. In both cases, the instruction is the same: a court is convened and witnesses are to testify to the violation. If the man is convicted, then the whole adult population is to join in the execution by stoning of the guilty defendant. That is the outcome in both episodes: the community has exercised its proper role as enforcer of the covenant rules, the violator has been punished, the covenant has been upheld, and the relationship between Yahweh and his people has been restored.

This pair of stories appears in what scholars believe to be the same literary source (P), deals specifically if not explicitly with successive commandments of the Decalogue, and supplies rules and procedures for dealing with violations of the commandment, information lacking in the Ten Commandments themselves. In regard to subject matter and specific detail of treatment, the two episodes in Leviticus 24 and Numbers 15 (the third and fourth books corresponding to the third and fourth commandments) are unique in the whole Hebrew Bible and there are no other stories like them, spelling out the specific violation along with prescribing the necessary punishment, dealing directly with blasphemy and Sabbath-breaking. They also form a distinctive pair in comparison with the rest of the commandments in the Decalogue.

The Ten Commandments are commonly divided in half between the two tables of stone on which they were incised. As we mentioned when discussing the sixth commandment, in each table we find two pairs of commandments, followed by a single recapitulating injunction, relating to the preceding sets of commandments. Finally, the two single commandments form a distinctive pair of their own. In their way, the last commandments in each table (numbers five and ten) serve to bind them all together and consolidate the basic obligations under the covenant, as for example, the summary of the Law attributed to Jesus in the Gospels: two pronouncements from the Torah (Deuteronomy 6:4–5 and Leviticus 9:8), one stressing one's duty toward God (the first table), and the other one's responsibility toward humankind (the second table).[15]

Numbers five and ten clearly stand apart from the others. Just as numbers three and four form a pair, so do numbers six and seven, eight and nine, and, as we have already seen, so do numbers one and two. In the decalogues in Exodus and Deuteronomy, the pairings are contiguous and consecutive, but even if we followed a different order, as we have with numbers six, seven, and eight, the pairings are still visible and emphatic. Thus in numbers six and seven we have the same setting and the same process of judicial inquiry and decision making. Moreover, behind both crimes is the powerful motivating force of covetousness, more precisely defined as greed (in the case of Achan recorded in Joshua 7) and lust (in the case of the gang rape and murder of the Levite's concubine in Judges 19). While the specific outcomes are different, both of these episodes belong to the post-Mosaic and premonarchic era, when the tribal confederation provided both governmental and juridical authority, especially when intertribal conflicts occurred. And the resolution in each case requires the tribal league to act in a concerted fashion against the malefactor, whether an individual, gang, or whole tribe.

Similarity in framework and atmosphere, as well as in some striking details, is true of the final pair (numbers eight and nine). In the narratives relating these episodes, both criminal violations occur during the period of the monarchy, one in Judah (the united kingdom) and one in Israel (the northern kingdom). Both principal violators are kings, and both cases involve women in their criminal activity, and in each case the woman in question is or will be the queen. While the details vary greatly and show that episodes are entirely independent of each other, the compiler/editor has organized and shaped them to fit into the larger pattern of *command* → *command violation* → *consequence,* which controls the entire narrative from Genesis through Kings. In both cases, the initial criminal violation of one of the commandments is compounded by another violation (murder of an innocent man), and in the latter instance, a third violation (theft). Nothing neat or simple in either case, but the criminal behavior builds to a climax, after which the end for each nation and the covenant community as a whole is inevitable.

In the case of King David, the initial violation is adultery with Bathsheba, the wife of another man, Uriah the Hittite. After the failure of various attempts to cover up the crime, or at least dissipate and obscure the incriminating evidence, David is driven in desperation to exercise his royal authority to arrange for Uriah's death in battle, thereby compounding adultery with murder; and in the end he marries the widow. In the process, David involves his henchman and nephew, Joab, the commander of the army, in this plot.

In the second instance (the ninth commandment), the initial crime is the bearing of false testimony against Naboth by witnesses who are hired for this purpose by the elders of Jezreel at the instigation of Jezebel, the wife and loyal helpmeet of the covetous King Ahab. The testimony of these false witnesses leads to the judicial murder of Naboth, compounding two direct violations of the Decalogue. In the end, Ahab takes possession of property that does not belong to him, so theft is added to the list of transgressions. There is a dramatic buildup as we approach the end of the table of commandments, with a double violation of number eight (adultery and murder) and a triple violation in number nine (false witness, murder, and theft). But in every case, both in this pair and earlier, it is the first violation that links the episode with the countdown of the commandments, and specifically with the Decalogue.

Once again, the motivation for the criminal undertaking is found in the last commandment about coveting. In the case of David it was covetousness expressed as lust (i.e., desiring his neighbor's wife), while in the case of Ahab, it was the same sin expressed as greed (i.e., the desire for his neighbor's property). In both cases, kings desired and took what did not rightfully belong to them, and in the process of securing the neighbor's wife or his property, they violated not only the specific commandments relating to wives (adultery) and property (theft) but others as well (including murder and false witness).

The commandments of the second table, therefore, form integral pairs (numbers six and seven, and numbers eight and nine) and together form a foursome, which, in turn, is explicated and interpreted by the Tenth Commandment. This final prohibition explores the interior motivation and intention in dealing with a fellow human being, often a neighbor, though the neighborhood has no geographical limit. In all four cases, the sinful intent underlying the criminal action that follows is illegitimate desire: coveting, expressed principally in two ways: greed for property and lust for persons. Thus, according to the order in the narratives (our count), numbers six and nine (Achan in the Book of Joshua, and Ahab in the Book of Kings) reflect greed, while numbers seven and eight (the men of Gibeah of Benjamin and King David) reflect lust.

If we were to follow the order of the canonical decalogues (Exodus 20 and Deuteronomy 5), then we would find numbers six and seven (murder and adultery) relating to persons, and numbers eight and nine (theft and false witness) relating to property, while the illustrative stories would show the connection in each specific instance. In every case, all four commandments and the stories belong together, and all are interpreted as examples of criminal actions produced by the covetousness prohibited in the Tenth Commandment. Coveting, not itself a crime but a sin, lies at the root of the four preceding prohibited criminal actions, and thus the Tenth Commandment pulls together the commandments of the second table and gives it its rationale.

In a similar fashion, the Fifth Commandment relates to the preceding group of four commandments and provides a setting or framework for their presentation. First, we note that the Fifth Commandment—in the fifth and middle book of the Primary History—like the Tenth Commandment, has no illustrative story associated with it. What we have instead is a hypothetical case, a casuistic formulation, well known throughout the Bible and in numerous Near Eastern legal inscriptions and documents (the famous Code of Hammurapi is only one example). The formulation follows a standard pattern: "If someone does such and such, then this is how you deal with the crime and the criminal."

As already explained, there is a close connection between an incident that gives rise to a precedent and hence a legal principle, and a precedent or principle that derives from such a case and then is applied to other cases of a similar nature. Real and hypothetical cases are different aspects and stages of the same process, and both types can and do exist side by side. The same legal principle can be expressed or embodied in either fashion. An event in which a case is decided can be generalized in hypothetical terms and applied to a whole class of similar episodes, while the reverse can also occur, where a hypothetical case is illustrated by an actual event and subsequently is used as a precedent in adjudicating future cases.

In the case of the Fifth Commandment on honoring one's parents, emphasis has properly been placed on the behavior of the children in regard to instructions or orders given by parents. While the general and specific obligations of children even into their own maturity are given priority, there is a corresponding responsibility or obligation of parents to their children, which, if not spelled out in detail, is nevertheless universally understood and accepted in the world of the Bible. Unless parents fulfill their manifest responsibility to care for, nurture, and otherwise prepare their children for life as adults, from birth through infancy and childhood, as well as adolescence until maturity, it would be fruitless to require those same children to be or do anything at all, surely not to be obedient to and honor the parents who must bear the original responsibility in relation to their children.

In order to understand the full measure of the commandment, we must ask what lies behind the demand for honor and obedience in terms of parental responsibility and activity. A reciprocal or two-way relationship is involved, and whatever is required of one party has to be understood in terms of what the other has done or is expected to do. The same reasoning applies to fellow human beings in the second table of commandments, namely, what is required of those who have and exercise a claim on the behavior of others. In other words, there is a Golden Rule of reciprocity, not always expressed but always implied or inferred.

The same is particularly true of parents and children. While the demand on and the expectation of children in the commandment is almost total, the corresponding and prior responsibility of the parents is of equal measure. The degree to which parents fulfill their responsibility toward children serves as the measure of the obligation and obedience that children may be expected to show their parents. Failure on the part of parents in their responsibility does not relieve children of their obligation to the parents, but it certainly will affect the ongoing relationship and the outcomes. Contrariwise, success on the part of the parents should produce appropriate compliance with the basic requirements of the commandment. The relationship between the parties and the reciprocity of their behaviors are affirmed, but the exact nature of the involvement and how one affects the other is hard to determine. It remains, however, to emphasize the importance of parental initiation and activity as the primary component in the foundation of this commandment and of all of the commandments taken together.

For this prior parental responsibility, we look to the formulation in Deuteronomy 6:4–7:

Hear, O Israel, The Lord is our God, the Lord is One. And you shall love the Lord your God with all your heart and with all your soul and with all your strength. And these words that I am commanding you today shall be upon your heart. And you shall teach them incisively to your children, and you shall speak of them when you sit down in your house, and when you walk in the way, and when you lie down and when you rise up.

The instruction for children follows after the Decalogue itself (Deuteronomy 5) and immediately after the Great Commandment in Deuteronomy 6. For ample expansion of this parental obligation, we look to the Book of Proverbs, much of which consists of the instructions of wise and noble parents to their children.

While we take for granted parental responsibility to provide food and clothing, shelter, and guidance in the way of life, the emphasis here and elsewhere in the Bible is on the transmission and inculcation of fundamental religious truths, i.e., the faith and obligations of the covenant, as for example, the Decalogue ramifications in the different legal codes of the Hebrew Bible. It is precisely this religious instruction that is to be heeded, and children honor their parents by heeding it.

By providing for the participants in their mutual and reciprocal engagement in the proper worship and service of God, the Fifth Commandment encompasses the preceding four commandments as a group. For every individual and the community as a whole, the role and responsibility of parents—the mother is specifically included along with the father—are indispensable as transmitters of the tradition and inculcators of the covenant terms and requirements, the rules governing membership in the holy congregation, and the behavior of each individual member. Thus, the preceding commandments in their pairs find their rightful place and function in the instructions given by parents to their children: first about Yahweh's nature and works, and then the obligation to worship and serve Yahweh alone.

The Fifth Commandment also points ahead to rules governing individual and community relationships. Once again, it is parental instruction, whether by formal teaching or by example, usually both, that applies to both tables: to the worship and service of God, on the one hand, and to the complex interrelationships of human beings, on the other. The revelation concerning these matters originates with God, but must come to human beings through human means, and the designated deliverers of this vital and indispensable nourishment are the parents specified in the Fifth Commandment. The emphasis of the Commandment is positive—honoring one's parents—in contrast with the negative tone throughout the Decalogue. In the context of the parental role and by reference to the many places in which parents fulfill their role as nurturers of their children, honoring one's parents means obedience and conformity not only in routine matters of family living, but specifically and emphatically in regard to the larger issues of true faith and worship of God, along with right behavior in all human relationships.

The Fifth Commandment finds its complement in the Tenth Commandment, which warns against the chief corrupting influence in human existence and the greatest hindrance to seeking to honor one's parents by scrupulous observance of all the commandments and the accompanying rules and regulations, which make for the fullness of life in the covenant community.

Tying Together the Loose Ends of Our Scarlet Thread

In the Primary History, the first true biography of a people recorded anywhere in the world, we can perceive a structural pattern, simple in conception, more complex in expression, but one that encompasses the entire work from beginning to end and permeates all of its parts. The Decalogue, in both places in the Hebrew Bible (another instance of pairing: one proclamation at the beginning of the wilderness wandering and the other at the end), constitutes the point of departure and the pivot or fulcrum on which the whole narrative hangs. That narrative is the account of the covenant relationship between Yahweh, the God, and Israel, his people, played out in time and space from the heroic and historic beginnings at Sinai/Horeb to the final ending in disaster, destruction, and captivity six hundred years later. I also showed that the overall design, while simple, nevertheless required the careful, purposeful organization of the narrative material into a coherent and cohesive scheme governing the movement of the story from beginning to end. The story is that of repeated violations of the covenant terms and persistent rebellion against the Lord of the covenant until the inevitable final punishment was inflicted on the people of the covenant and the national enterprise was terminated violently by the capture of the city of Jerusalem, the razing of the Temple, and the exile of the leading citizens.

All of this may be self-evident as the narrative unfolds itself through the nine books of the Torah and the Former Prophets (the Primary History) of the Hebrew Bible. But in addition to the general scheme, about which all may agree, we have uncovered a hidden outline or thread that runs through the whole, spelling out the countdown to oblivion for this nation: book by book, commandment by commandment, dramatic episode after dramatic episode, from start to finish, from Sinai to Jerusalem and beyond, the Nine Commandments are broken, divine patience has been exhausted, and the instruments of divine punishment, the Assyrian and Babylonian armies, have overwhelmed the two nations as the narration hurries along to its denouement at the end of the Book of Kings. So the experiment in living as the people of God under the laws of the covenant came to a tragic end.

Every detail does not fit neatly into this scheme. It couldn't. The one responsible for the pattern of the scarlet thread was working with diverse traditions spanning hundreds of years and deriving from different segments within Israelite society—royal scribes, priests, prophets. Yet, despite the complexity of the development and transmission of these traditions, the evidence is overwhelming: this scarlet thread of commandment violations, which has remained hidden for more than two millennia, was the result of an intelligent mind, a Master Weaver/Editor, who put it all together for the edification and enlightenment of those who had survived the crisis of 586 B.C.E.—and not just for them, but for all who share in this tradition and belong to the household of faith.

Abbreviations

ABD	D. N. Freedman (ed.), *Anchor Bible Dictionary*
ANET	J. B. Pritchard (ed.), *Ancient Near Eastern Texts Relating to the Old Testament* (3rd ed.)
BA	*Biblical Archaeologist*
BASOR	*Bulletin of the American Schools of Oriental Research*
BARev	*Biblical Archaeology Review*
CBQ	*Catholic Biblical Quarterly*
HUCA	*Hebrew Union College Annual*
IDBSup	*Interpreter's Dictionary of the Bible* (Supplement)
JBL	*Journal of Biblical Literature*
JSOT	*Journal for the Study of the Old Testament*
KTU	M. Dietrich, O. Loretz, and J. Sanmartin, *Die keilalphabetischen Texte aus Ugarit: Einschliesslich der keilalphabetischen Texte ausserhalb Ugarits I, Transkription*
RQ	*Revue de Qumran*
SBLDS	Society of Biblical Literature Dissertation Series
TDOT	G. J. Botterweck and H. Ringgren (eds.), *Theological Dictionary of the Old Testament 1–5*
VT	*Vetus Testamentum*

Notes

Foreword

1. Reprinted in *Divine Commitment and Human Obligation*, vol. 1, pp. 43–49.

2. Ibid., 496–520.

3. Also reprinted in *Divine Commitment*, 457–69.

4. David N. Freedman, *The Unity of the Hebrew Bible* (Ann Arbor, MI: The University of Michigan Press, 1991).

5. Francis I. Andersen and David Freedman, *Amos* (AB24A; New York: Doubleday, 1989), 638–79. Reprinted in *Divine Commitment*, 409–46.

6. Ibid., 645–46.

7. Freedman, *The Unity of the Hebrew Bible*, 6–7.

8. Ibid., 8.

9. Ibid., 9.

10. See p. 168 of this book.

11. A. B. Beck, A. H. Bartelt, P. R. Raabe, C. A. Franke, eds. *Fortunate the Eyes That See: David Noel Freedman Festschrift*. (Grand Rapids, MI: Eerdmans, 1995), 601.

Introduction

1. The command to "be fruitful and multiply" (Genesis 1:28), although appearing earlier in the biblical record, is not earlier than the command not to eat of the fruit (Genesis 2:17), since the command to refrain from the tree is given *before* the woman is created, whereas the command to procreate is given after the creation of both the man and the woman. Actually, most scholars view Genesis 1 and 2 as competing accounts of creation. However, it is also possible to view them as com-

plementary—the first giving an overview of creation, the second providing a more detailed description of humankind's beginnings. In either case, in the text as we have it, the command not to eat from the tree is logically prior to the command to procreate.

2. Genesis 3:9.

3. Genesis 4:9a.

4. Genesis 3:16.

5. Genesis 4:12.

6. What the "mark" might have been or where it may have been placed is a mystery. Perhaps the mark (Hebrew: *'ot)* is to be understood as a symbol or word (perhaps even the Divine name) placed upon Cain so that it was visible to others (i.e., the forehead; cf. Ezekiel 9:4–6). The important point for our purposes is that God shows Cain mercy although he is undeserving.

7. In both Genesis 3:24 and 4:14, the word for "to drive" comes from the Hebrew root *garash*.

8. Hebrew: *'aseret hadevarim*.

9. On the prevalence and significance of the numbers seven, ten, and twelve (and others), see J. Friberg, "Numbers and Counting," *ABD* (1992) 4:1139–46.

10. The power of Exodus imagery to inspire has been visible in a number of movements seeking freedom or autonomy from oppression. The American colonies' own fight for independence was likened to Israel's independence from Egypt. In fact, the king of England was called the British Pharaoh, and it was Ben Franklin's proposal that the seal of the United States picture Moses holding up his staff and the Egyptians drowning in the Red Sea, with the motto: "Resistance to tyrants is obedience to God."

11. Exodus 12:37–42; 13:18b–22.

12. Exodus 14:5–7.

13. Exodus 14:9.

14. A similar humor is present in the Israelites' recollection of how good things were in Egypt (Exodus 16:3 and Numbers 11:4–6).

15. Exodus 15. For a discussion of this song, its content and its antiquity, see F. M. Cross and D. N. Freedman, *Studies in Ancient Yahwistic Poetry* (Grand Rapids, MI: Eerdmans; Livonia, MI: Dove, 1997), 31–45. Reprinted from *Studies in Ancient Yahwistic Poetry* (SBLDS 21 Missoula, MT: Scholars, 1975).

16. Exodus 15:24.

17. Numbers 13:25–26.

18. Genesis 6:2. For a discussion of theories about the Nephilim, see R. S. Hess, "Nephilim," *ABD* 4:1072–73.

19. Genesis 6:4.

20. Numbers 14:12.

21. Numbers 14:19.

22. See, for example, Genesis 15:13–16, where Israel's enslavement, release, and return are foretold by God to Abraham.

23. Deuteronomy 28:3–14.

24. Deuteronomy 28:16–68. The amount of space devoted to the curses Israel would endure if disobedient to God's commands is striking when compared to the blessings they would enjoy if obedient.

25. Exodus 20:3–6; Deuteronomy 5:7–10.

The First & Second Commandments

1. See the Introduction for a discussion of the different numbering systems for the Ten Commandments.

2. The Hebrew word *lipne,* like the English "before" or "in front of," can refer to location or priority. While the first commandment no doubt refers to priority, in a cultic context that which symbolizes the deity's presence (i.e., the idol or, in the case of Yahweh, the Ark) would also be given locative priority in the Temple. Thus, the Ark of the Covenant has priority of place in the Holy Place of the Tabernacle and Temple.

3. For an account of the discovery and significance of the Ras-Shamra texts for biblical studies, see P. C. Craigie, *Ugarit and the Old Testament* (Grand Rapids, MI: Eerdmans, 1983).

4. "The Baal Cycle," *KTU* 1.1–6.

5. The account of Marduk's victory over the forces of chaos is found in the Babylonian account of creation entitled *Enuma Elish.* This cosmic drama was reenacted each year at the Babylonian New Year's festival *(ANET,* 331–34).

6. On the relationship between El and Yahweh, see F. M. Cross, *Canaanite Myth and Hebrew Epic* (Cambridge: Harvard University Press, 1973), 44–75.

7. For a more complete discussion of the names for God and their development, see D. N. Freedman, "Divine Names and Titles in Early Hebrew Poetry," in *Magnalia Dei: The Mighty Acts of God,* eds. F. M. Cross, W. E. Lemke, and P. D. Miller, Jr. (Garden City, NY: Doubleday, 1976), 55–107 and "The Name of the God of Moses," *JBL* 79 (1960),

151–56. See also E. A. Knauf, "Yahwe," *VT* 34 (1984), 467–72 and R. Abba, "The Divine Name Yahweh," *JBL* 80 (1961), 320–28.

8. For the possible origin and meaning of Shaddai, see K. Koch, "Šaddaj. Zum Verhältnis zwischen israelitischer Monolatrie und nord-west-semitischem Polytheismus," *VT* 26 (1976), 299–332.

9. See, for example, the discussion in *TDOT* 1:242–61.

10. The name Yahweh is known to Abraham (Genesis 12:8), Isaac (Genesis 26:22), and Jacob (Genesis 27:20).

11. For a useful introduction to the development of and evidence for the Documentary Hypothesis, see R. E. Friedman, *Who Wrote the Bible?* (New York: Summit Books, 1987).

12. J. Wellhausen, *Prolegomena zur Geschichte Israels* (Edinburgh: A. & C. Black, 1885. Reprinted, Gloucester, MA: Peter Smith, 1973; German, 1878).

13. For a survey of alternative theories to the Documentary Hypothesis, see R. N. Whybray, *The Making of the Pentateuch* (JSOTSup 53; Sheffield: JSOT Press, 1987).

14. The revelation of the name Yahweh occurs in Exodus 3 (E) and 6 (P), respectively.

15. For an informative as well as provocative analysis of goddess worship in Israel and the ancient Near East, see T. Frymer-Kensky, *In the Wake of the Goddesses: Women, Culture, and the Biblical Transformation of Pagan Myth* (New York: Free Press; Toronto: Maxwell Macmillan Canada; New York: Maxwell Macmillan Int'l, 1992).

16. The Queen of Heaven is mentioned only in the book of Jeremiah (7:18; 44:17, 18, 19, 25). For a discussion of her identification, see P. C. Schmitz, "Queen of Heaven," *ABD* 5:586–88.

17. For discussions of Yahweh's relationship to Asherah in light of the Kuntillet ᶜAjrud inscriptions, see Z. Meshel, "Did Yahweh Have a Consort? The New Religious Inscriptions from Sinai," *BARev* 5/2 (1979), 24–34; W. G. Dever, "Asherah, Consort of Yahweh? New Evidence from Kuntillet ᶜAjrud," *BASOR* 255 (1984), 21–37; D. N. Freedman, "Yahweh of Samaria and His Asherah," *BA* (1987), 241–49.

18. 1 Kings 18:19.

19. The Hebrew word "image" *(tselem)* to describe humankind's likeness to God in Genesis 1:26–27 is the same word to describe idols (cf., for example, Numbers 33:52 and 2 Kings 11:18).

20. D. B. Redford, "Apis," *ABD* 1:278–79.

21. I. Lewy, "The Late Assyro-Babylonian Cult of the Moon and Its Culmination at the Time of Nabonidus," *HUCA* 19 (1945–46), 405–89.

22. Genesis 11:31.

23. *KTU* 1.4 II:10; 1.3 III:29.

24. A. Mazar, "The 'Bull Site'—An Iron Age I Open Cult Place," *BASOR* 247 (1982), 27–42.

25. 1 Kings 12:26–33.

26. It is widely held that the account of the Golden Calf was written with the sin of Jeroboam in mind (see M. Aberbach and L. Smolar, "Aaron, Jeroboam, and the Golden Calves," *JBL* 86 [1967], 129–40), the purpose being to denigrate Aaron and condemn Jeroboam. Hence, the reference to "gods" (plural) in the Exodus narrative, although Aaron only constructs one god (calf), connects Aaron's sin with Jeroboam's, who did build two calves—one at Dan and another at Bethel. In fact, both Aaron and Jeroboam are presented as saying the same thing upon its/their construction: "These are your gods, O Israel, that brought you out of the land of Egypt" (Exodus 32:4; 1 Kings 12:28).

27. Exodus 32:17.

28. Exodus 15.

29. Genesis 26:6–11.

30. Genesis 12:10–20; 20:1–18.

31. Genesis 20:3.

32. Exodus 32:8.

33. Exodus 32:9–14.

34. Exodus 32:16 emphasizes that the tablets Moses carried "were the work of God and the writing was the writing of God."

The Third Commandment

1. P. Kalluveettil, *Declaration and Covenant: A Comprehensive Review of Covenant Formulae from the Old Testament and the Ancient Near East* (AnBib 88; Rome: Biblical Institute, 1982); D. J. McCarthy, *Treaty and Covenant: A Study in Form in the Ancient Oriental Documents and in the Old Testament* (AnBib 21A; Rome: Biblical Institute, 1978).

2. G. E. Mendenhall, "Covenant Forms in Israelite Tradition," *BA* 17 (1954), 50–76; K. Baltzer, *The Covenant Formulary in Old Testament, Jewish, and Early Christian Writings* (Philadelphia: Fortress and Oxford: Blackwell, 1971. German, 1964).

3. See pp. 27–29.

4. The sacredness of the divine name can even be seen in the preservation of the paleo-Hebrew characters in many of the Dead Sea Scrolls.

5. For a discussion of the rationale behind the purity laws of Leviticus, see D. P. Wright, "Unclean and Clean (Old Testament)," *ABD* 6:739–41.

6. Numbers 15:32–36.

7. See Deuteronomy 28:58 for a possible second example of "the Name" (Hebrew: *hashem*) in place of the actual divine name.

8. Job 2:9.

9. Job 2:10.

10. Job 1:5.

11. Leviticus 24:10. Note that Ishmael is also of mixed parentage: Abraham, a Hebrew, and Hagar, an Egyptian.

12. Exodus 12:12; Numbers 33:4.

13. See, for example, Numbers 15:30–31.

14. Leviticus 24:10.

15. For the account of Moses slaying the Egyptian and his flight to Midian, see Exodus 2:11–15.

16. Exodus 2:13–14.

17. Exodus 2:13.

18. For the murder of Amnon by his brother Absalom and Absalom's self-imposed exile, see 2 Samuel 13:23–39.

19. Leviticus 24:11.

20. Exodus 32:26–29.

The Fourth Commandment

1. For a discussion of the possible origins of and reasons for the Sabbath, see G. F. Hasel, "Sabbath," *ABD* 5:849–56.

2. For two of the early reports (in English) of the Dead Sea Scrolls' discovery, see W. F. Albright, *BASOR* 110 (April 1948), 1–3 and G. E. Wright, "A Sensational Discovery," *BA* (May 1948), 21–23. For a more general introduction to the Dead Sea Scrolls and the Qumran community, see F. M. Cross, *The Ancient Library of Qumran and Modern Biblical Studies* (Garden City, NY: Doubleday, 1958); J. T. Milik, *Ten Years of Discovery in the Wilderness of Judaea* (London: SCM, 1959).

3. See especially Damascus Document (CD) X–XII. See also the discussion of S. T. Kimbrough, "The Concept of the Sabbath at Qumran," *RQ* 20 (1966), 483–502.

4. A. F. Johns, "The Military Strategy of Sabbath Attacks on the Jews," *VT* 13 (1963), 482–86.

5. See Jeremiah 52:5–8.

6. 1 Maccabees 2:38–41.

7. Matthew 12:11.

8. CD XI:13–14.

9. *Hagigah* 1:8.

10. Note the name "Shabbethai" in Ezekiel 10:15 and Nehemiah 8:7 and 11:16.

11. For a general discussion of the relationship between Jesus' teaching and worldview and that of Judaism, see G. Vermes, *The Religion of Jesus the Jew* (Minneapolis: Fortress, 1993).

12. The text moves from describing what to do in the case of unintentional and intentional sins (Numbers 15:22–31) to the account of the Sabbath violation (Numbers 15:32–36). This account is then followed by laws regarding the wearing of tassels (Numbers 15:37–40).

13. In Leviticus 24 the blasphemer is referred to as "a son of an Israelite woman" and in Numbers 15 the Sabbath violator is simply referred to as "a man."

The Fifth Commandment

1. Exodus 24:16.

2. Exodus 40:34–35.

3. Hebrew: *qaran*.

4. R. Mellinkoff, *The Horned Moses in Medieval Art and Thought* (Berkeley: UC Press, 1970).

5. W. H. C. Propp, "The Skin of Moses' Face—Transfigured or Disfigured?" *CBQ* 49 (1987), 375–76.

6. Leviticus 10:6.

7. See, for example, Exodus 14:11–12; 15:24; 16:2–3; 17:2; etc.

8. Numbers 11:10–14.

9. Numbers 11:15.

10. Exodus 17:5–6.

11. Numbers 20:2–8.

12. Numbers 20:8.

13. W. C. Propp, "The Rod of Aaron and the Sin of Moses," *JBL* 107 (1988), 19–26.

14. Numbers 16:1–11.

15. Numbers 17:10.

16. Numbers 20:10.

17. Numbers 20:10.

18. Numbers 20:24.

19. Numbers 20:27–28.

20. Isaiah 65:2.

21. Cf. Jeremiah 6:28.
22. Cf. Isaiah 1:23.
23. Cf. Nehemiah 9:29–30.
24. Ephesians 6:1–3.
25. Deuteronomy 29–30.

The Sixth Commandment

1. Josephus, *The Antiquities of the Jews,* 3.5.5.
2. Philo, *De Decalogo,* 10.36.
3. Luke 18:20.
4. Matthew 19:18; Mark 10:19.
5. Jeremiah 7:8–11.
6. Judges 14.
7. 2 Samuel 15:6; 1 Samuel 31.
8. See for example, R. E. Friedman, *Who Wrote the Bible?,* 125–27.
9. Friedman, *Who Wrote the Bible?,* 144–49.
10. For additional information on this seal and the seals of other biblical personages, see T. Schneider, "Six Biblical Signatures," *BARev* (July/August 1991), 27–33.
11. Jeremiah 7:9.
12. Job 1:1.
13. 1 Samuel 14:38–39.
14. For more information, see J. Lindblom, "Lot-Casting in the Old Testament," *VT* 12 (1962) 164–78.
15. Exodus 22:1.
16. 1 Samuel 31:2–6.
17. 2 Samuel 4:7.
18. 2 Samuel 21.
19. 2 Samuel 6:23.
20. 1 Samuel 20:15–17.
21. Joshua 22.

The Seventh Commandment

1. For a more detailed study of literary patterns in Judges, see R. G. Boling, *Judges (AB* 6a; Garden City, NY: Doubleday, 1975), 29–38.
2. For more information on the role of judges in the Hebrew Bible and ancient Near East, see Boling, *Judges, AB* 6a, 5–6.
3. Judges 8:22.

4. For a popular and fascinating study of Richard III, see J. Tey, *The Daughter of Time* (New York: Macmillan, 1952).

5. Judges 1:34.

6. Judges 19:22.

7. Judges 19:23.

8. Judges 19:24.

9. Note the similarities between this story and that of Sodom and Gommorah in Genesis 19.

10. Judges 19.

The Eighth Commandment

1. Genesis 17:6.

2. 1 Samuel 4–6.

3. 1 Samuel 13:9.

4. 1 Samuel 15:3.

5. For further information, see R. Beckwith, *The Old Testament Canon of the New Testament Church and Its Background in Early Judaism* (Grand Rapids, MI: Eerdmans, 1985); James A. Sanders, "Canon," *ABD* 1:837–52.

6. See D. N. Freedman, *The Unity of the Hebrew Bible* (Ann Arbor: University of Michigan Press, 1993).

7. E. A. Goodfriend, "Adultery," *ABD* 1:82–86.

8. 1 Samuel 1:1–5.

9. 2 Samuel 13:23–33.

10. 2 Samuel 18:14–15.

11. 2 Samuel 12:10.

The Ninth Commandment

1. Deuteronomy 19:15.

2. Genesis 4:9.

3. Genesis 26:6.

4. Genesis 27.

5. Genesis 20:12.

6. Joshua 2:4–5.

7. 1 Kings 16:32–33.

8. For additional information on the jubilee, see C.J.H. Wright, "Jubilee, Year of," *ABD* 3: 1025–30.

9. 1 Kings 21:4.

10. 1 Kings 21:7.

11. 1 Kings 21:13.

12. 1 Kings 21:16.

13. 1 Kings 21:19.

14. 1 Kings 21:29.

15. 1 Kings 22:38.

16. 2 Kings 9:30–37.

17. For an English translation of the Assyrian text, see J. Pritchard, *Ancient Near Eastern Texts Relating to the Old Testament* (Princeton: Princeton University Press, 1969), 287–88.

18. Herodotus, *Histories* 2.141.

19. 2 Kings 22:33.

20. 2 Kings 22.

21. 2 Kings 22:13.

22. A fuller treatment of Megiddo as battlefield for the Apocalypse is found in J. Paulien, "Armageddon," *ABD* 1:394–95.

23. 2 Kings 24:1.

24. 2 Kings 24:12–15.

25. 2 Kings 25:18–21.

26. 2 Kings 25:7.

27. 2 Kings 25:9.

28. 2 Kings 25:27–30.

The Tenth Commandment?

1. Matthew 5:27–28.

2. Field and vineyard are parallel in Exodus 22:5; Leviticus 25:3–4; Numbers 20:17; 21:22; Proverbs 24:30, etc.

Conclusion

1. Genesis 12:1–3.

2. Genesis 12:10–20.

3. Genesis 23.

4. See especially Deuteronomy 29–31.

5. 2 Kings 17:7, 35–38; 22:17.

6. See pp. 15–16.

7. See the discussion on pp. 85–96.

8. D. N. Freedman and S. Mandell, *The Relationship Between Herodotus' History and Primary History* (South Florida Studies in the History of Judaism 60; Atlanta: Scholars Press, 1993).

9. D. N. Freedman, *The Unity of the Hebrew Bible* (Ann Arbor: University of Michigan Press, 1991).

10. Exodus 21–23.

11. Cf. Exodus 22:28.

12. Job 1:5.

13. Job 2:5.

14. Job 2:9.

15. Cf. Matthew 22:34–40 and parallels in Mark 12:28–34 and Luke 10:25–28.

Select Bibliography

Abba, R. "The Divine Name Yahweh," *JBL* 80 (1961) 320–28.

Aberbach, M. and L. Smolar. "Aaron, Jeroboam and the Golden Calves," *JBL* 86 (1967) 129–40.

Aharoni, Y. *The Land of the Bible: A Historical Geography* (Philadelphia: Westminster, 1979).

Albright, W. F. *From the Stone Age to Christianity* (Baltimore: Johns Hopkins, 1946).

———. *The Biblical Period from Abraham to Ezra* (New York: Harper & Row, Publishers, 1949).

Andersen, Francis I., and David Noel Freedman. *Amos* (AB 24A; New York: Doubleday, 1989).

Baltzer, K. *The Covenant Formulary in Old Testament, Jewish, and Early Christian Writings* (Philadelphia: Fortress, and Oxford: Blackwell, 1971. German, 1964).

Beck, A. B., A. H. Bartelt, P. R. Raabe, C. A. Franke, eds. *Fortunate the Eyes That See. David Noel Freedman Festschrift* (Grand Rapids, MI: Eerdmans, 1995).

Beckwith, R. *The Old Testament Canon of the New Testament Church and Its Background in Early Judaism* (Grand Rapids, MI: Eerdmans, 1985).

Boling, R. G. *Judges* (AB 6a; Garden City, NY: Doubleday, 1975).

——— and G. E. Wright. *Joshua* (AB 6; Garden City, NY: Doubleday, 1982).

Botterweck, G. J., H. Ringgren, and H. J. Fabry, eds. *Theological Dictionary of the Old Testament* (Grand Rapids, 1974).

Bright, J. *Jeremiah* (AB 21; New York: Doubleday, 1965).

———. *A History of Israel* (Philadelphia: Westminster Press, 1981).

Brodsky, H. "Bethel," *ABD* (New York: Doubleday, 1992) 1:710–11.

Burney, C. F. *Notes on the Hebrew Text of the Books of Kings* (Oxford: Clarendon, 1903).

Callaway, J. A. *The Early Bronze Age Citadel and Lower City at Ai et-Tell* (Cambridge: ASOR, 1980).

Campbell, A. *Of Prophets and Kings: A Late Ninth-Century Document 1 Samuel 1–2 Kings 10* (CBQMS 17; Washington: The Catholic Biblical Association of America, 1986).

Cheyne, T. K. *Founders of Old Testament Criticism* (London: Methuen, 1893).

Cogan, M. and H. Tadmor. *2 Kings* (AB 11; Garden City, NY: Doubleday, 1988).

Craigie, P. C. *Ugarit and the Old Testament* (Grand Rapids, MI: Eerdmans, 1983).

Cross, F. M. *The Ancient Library of Qumran and Modern Biblical Studies* (Garden City, NY: Doubleday, 1958).

———. *Canaanite Myth and Hebrew Epic* (Cambridge: Harvard University Press, 1973).

——— and D. N. Freedman. *Studies in Ancient Yahwistic Poetry* (Grand Rapids, MI: Eerdmans; Livonia, MI: Dove, 1997; reprinted from *Studies in Ancient Yahwistic Poetry;* SBLDS 21; Missoula, MT: Scholars, 1975).

de Vaux, R. *The Bible and the Ancient Near East* (New York: Doubleday, 1971).

Dever, W. G. "Asherah, Consort of Yahweh? New Evidence from Kuntillet ᶜAjrud," *BASOR* 255 (1984) 21–37.

Dietrich, M., O. Loretz, and J. Sanmartín. *Keilalphabetischen Texte aus Ugarit* (AOAT 24; Kevelaer and Neukirchen-Vluyn, 1976).

Driver, S. R. *Introduction to the Literature of the Old Testament* (New York: Charles Scribner's Sons, 1892).

Eissfeldt, O. *The Old Testament: An Introduction* (New York: Harper, 1965. German; Tübingen: Mohr, 1934).

Engnell, I. Trans. and ed. by J. T. Willis and H. Ringgren. *A Rigid Scrutiny. Critical Essays on the Old Testament* (Nashville: Abingdon, 1969).

Freedman, D. N. "The Name of the God of Moses," *JBL* 79 (1960) 151–56.

———. "Pentateuch," *IDB* (1962) 3:716–17.

———. "The Deuteronomic History," *IDBSup* (1976) 226–28.

———. "Divine Names and Titles in Early Hebrew Poetry," in *Magnalia Dei: The Mighty Acts of God,* eds. F. M. Cross, W. E. Lemke, and P. D. Miller, Jr. (Garden City, NY: Doubleday, 1976) 55–107.

———. "Yahweh of Samaria and His Asherah," *BA* (1987) 241–49.

———. *The Unity of the Hebrew Bible* (Ann Arbor: University of Michigan Press, 1991).

———, editor-in-chief. *The Anchor Bible Dictionary*. 6 vols. Assoc. Eds. Gary A. Herion, David F. Grof, John David Pleins. Managing Ed. Astrid B. Beck (New York: Doubleday, 1992).

———. and S. Mandell. *The Relationship Between Herodotus' History and Primary History* (South Florida Studies in the History of Judaism 60; Atlanta: Scholars Press, 1993).

———. and J. C. Geoghegan. " 'House of David' Is There!" *BARev* (March/April 1995).

———. John R. Huddlestun, editor. *Divine Commitment and Human Obligation*. Vol. 1: *Ancient Israelite History and Religion*. (Grand Rapids, MI: Eerdmans, 1997).

Friberg, J. "Numbers and Counting," *ABD* (1992) 4:1139–46.

Friedman, R. E. *The Exile and Biblical Narrative. The Formation of the Deuteronomistic and Priestly Works* (HSM 22. Chico: Scholars Press, 1981).

———. "From Egypt to Egypt: Dtr¹ and Dtr²," in *Traditions in Transformation: Turning Points in Biblical Faith*. Frank Moore Cross *Festschrift*. Eds. B. Halpern and J. D. Levenson (Winona Lake: Eisenbrauns, 1981) 167–92.

———. "Torah (Pentateuch)," *ABD* (1992) 6:612.

———. *Who Wrote the Bible?* (New York: Summit Books, 1987).

———. "The Deuteronomistic School," in *Fortunate the Eyes That See*. David Noel Freedman *Festschrift*. Eds. A. Beck, A. Bartelt, P. Raabe and C. Franke (Grand Rapids, MI: Eerdmans, 1995) 70–80.

———. *The Hidden Book in the Bible* (San Francisco: HarperCollins, 1998).

Frymer-Kensky, T. *In the Wake of the Goddesses: Women, Culture, and the Biblical Transformation of Pagan Myth* (New York: Free Press; Toronto: Maxwell Macmillan Canada; New York: Maxwell Macmillan Int'l, 1992).

Goodfriend, E. A. "Adultery," *ABD* (1992) 1:82–86.

Gottwald, N. K. *The Tribes of Yahweh: A Sociology of the Religion of Liberated Israel, 1250–1050* B.C.E. (Maryknoll, NY: Orbis, 1979).

———. *The Hebrew Bible—A Socio-Literary Introduction* (Philadelphia: Fortress Press, 1985).

Grant, R. M. and D. Tracy. *A Short History of the Interpretation of the Bible* (New York: Macmillan, 1963).

Gray, E. M. *Old Testament Criticism: Its Rise and Progress* (New York and London: Harper & Row, 1923).

Gray, J. *1 & 2 Kings* (OTL. Philadelphia: Westminster, 1970).

Halpern, B. *The Constitution of the Monarchy in Israel* (HSM 25; Chico: Scholars Press, 1981).

Hasel, G. F. "Sabbath," *ABD* (1992) 5:849–56.

Hess, R. S. "Nephilim," *ABD* (1992) 4:1072–73.

Johns, A. F. "The Military Strategy of Sabbath Attacks on the Jews," *VT* 13 (1963) 482–86.

Kalluveettil, P. *Declaration and Covenant: A Comprehensive Review of Covenant Formulae from the Old Testament and the Ancient Near East* (AnBib 88; Rome: Biblical Institute, 1982).

Kaufmann, Y. *The Religion of Israel*. Trans. M. Greenberg. (Chicago: Chicago University, 1960. Hebrew; Tel Aviv, 1937–47).

Kimbrough, S. T. "The Concept of the Sabbath at Qumran," *RQ* 20 (1966) 483–502.

Knauf, E. A. "Yahwe," *VT* 34 (1984) 467–72.

Levitt Kohn, R. "A New Heart and a New Soul: Ezekiel, the Exile and the Torah." Ph.D. dissertation (University of California, San Diego, 1997).

Levy, T. *The Archaeology of Society in the Holy Land* (New York: Facts on File, 1995).

Lewy, I. The Late Assyro-Babylonian Cult of the Moon and Its Culmination at the Time of Nabonidus," *HUCA* 19 (1945–46) 405–89.

Lindblom, J. "Lot-Casting in the Old Testament," *VT* 12 (1962) 164–78.

Lundbom, J. R. "Jeremiah, Book of," *ABD* (1992) 3:706–21.

———. "Jeremiah (Prophet)," *ABD* (1992) 3:686–90.

Mayes, A.D.H. *The Story of Israel Between Settlement and Exile. A Redactional Study of the Deuteronomistic History* (London: SCM, 1983).

Mazar, A. "The 'Bull Site'—An Iron Age I Open Cult Place," *BASOR* 247 (1982) 27–42.

McCarter, P. K. *I Samuel* (AB **8**; Garden City, NY: Doubleday, 1980).

McCarthy, D. J. *Treaty and Covenant: A Study in Form in the Ancient Oriental Documents and in the Old Testament* (AnBib 21A; Rome: Biblical Institute, 1978).

McKenzie, S. L. *The Trouble with Kings. The Composition of the Books of Kings in the Deuteronomistic History* (VTSup 42. Leiden: E. J. Brill, 1991).

Mellinkoff, R. *The Horned Moses in Medieval Art and Thought* (Berkeley: University of California Press, 1970).

Mendenhall, G. E. "Covenant Forms in Israelite Tradition," *BA* 17 (1954) 50–76.

Meshel, Z. "Did Yahweh Have a Consort? The New Religious Inscriptions from Sinai," *BARev* 5/2 (1979) 24–34.

Milgrom, J. *Leviticus 1–16* (AB 3; New York: Doubleday, 1991).

Milik, J. T. *Ten Years of Discovery in the Wilderness of Judaea* (London: SCM, 1959).

Miller, J. M. and J. H. Hayes. *A History of Ancient Israel and Judah* (Philadelphia: Westminster Press, 1986).

Montgomery, J. A. "Archival Data in the Book of Kings," *JBL* 53 (1934) 46–52.

Moore, G. F. *A Critical and Exegetical Commentary on Judges* (ICC. New York: Charles Scribner's Sons, 1906).

Nelson, R. D. *Joshua. A Commentary* (OTL. Louisville: Westminster John Knox, 1997).

Nicholson, E. W. *Deuteronomy and Tradition* (Philadelphia: Fortress Press, 1967).

———. *The Pentateuch in the Twentieth Century: The Legacy of Julius Wellhausen* (Oxford: Clarendon, 1998).

Noth, M. *The Deuteronomistic History* (JSOTSup 15. Sheffield: JSOT, 1981. German; Halle: Niemeyer, 1943).

Paulien, J. "Armageddon," *ABD* (1992) 1:394–95.

Peckham, B. *The Composition of the Deuteronomistic History* (HSM 35; Atlanta: Scholars, 1985).

———. *History and Prophecy History. The Development of Late Judean Literary Traditions* (New York: Doubleday, 1993).

Pfeiffer, R. H. *Introduction to the Old Testament* (New York: Harper & Row, Publishers, 1948).

Pritchard, J. B. *Ancient Near Eastern Texts Relating to the Old Testament* (Princeton: Princeton University Press, 1969).

Propp, W.H.C. "The Skin of Moses' Face—Transfigured or Disfigured?" *CBQ* 49 (1987) 375–76.

———. "The Rod of Aaron and the Sin of Moses," *JBL* 107 (1988) 19–26.

———. *Exodus.* (AB 2; Garden City, NY: Doubleday, 1999).

Redford, D. B. "Apis," *ABD* (1992) 1:278–79.

Rogerson, J. W. *Old Testament Criticism in the Nineteenth Century* (Philadelphia: Fortress Press, 1985).

Sanders, J. A. "Canon," *ABD* (1992) 1:837–52.

Schmitz, P. C. "Queen of Heaven," *ABD* (1992) 5:586–88.

Schneider, T. "Six Biblical Signatures," *BARev* (July/August 1991) 27–33.

Smalley, B. *The Study of the Bible in the Middle Ages* (Notre Dame: Notre Dame Press, 1964).

Soggin, A. *Judges. A Commentary* (OTL. London: SCM, 1981).

Speiser, E. A. *Genesis* (AB 1; New York: Doubleday, 1964).

Tey, J. *The Daughter of Time* (New York: Macmillan, 1952).

Tov, E. *Textual Criticism of the Hebrew Bible* (Minneapolis: Fortress Press, 1992).

Van Seters, J. *In Search of History. Historiography in the Ancient World and the Origins of Biblical History* (New Haven: Yale University, 1983).

Vermes, G. *The Religion of Jesus the Jew* (Minneapolis: Fortress Press, 1993).

———. *The Dead Sea Scrolls in English,* 4th ed. (New York: Penguin, 1995).

von Rad, G. *Studies in Deuteronomy.* (SBT 9. London: SCM, 1953. German; Göttingen: Vandenhoeck & Ruprecht, 1947).

Weinfeld, M. *Deuteronomy and the Deuteronomistic School* (New York: Oxford University Press, 1972).

———. *Deuteronomy 1–11* (AB 5; Garden City, NY: Doubleday, 1991).

Wellhausen, J. *Prolegomena to the History of Ancient Israel* (New York: Meridian Books, 1961).

Whybray, R. N. *The Making of the Pentateuch* (JSOTSup 53; Sheffield: JSOT Press, 1987).

Wright, C.J.H. "Jubilee, Year of," *ABD* (1992) 3:1025–30.

Wright, D. P. "Unclean and Clean (Old Testament)," *ABD* (1992) 6:739–41.

Wright, G. E. "A Sensational Discovery," *BA* (May 1948) 21–23.

Sources Index

General Index

©Timothy Mantoani

About the Author

David Noel Freedman has been General Editor and a contributing coauthor of the Anchor Bible series since its inception in 1956. He is a professor of the Hebrew Bible at the University of California, San Diego, and lives in La Jolla, California.